THE RED MAN COMETH

THE RED MAN COMETH

Geraldine Pengelly

ATHENA PRESS
LONDON

THE RED MAN COMETH

ISBN 1 84401 717 6

First Published 2006 by
ATHENA PRESS
Queen's House, 2 Holly Road
Twickenham TW1 4EG
United Kingdom

Printed for Athena Press

This book is dedicated to the memory of my dear mother and father,
Gladys and Henry John,
in celebration of their lives on this earth.

Also, to my three lovely children, Lesley, Paul and Mark.
And not forgetting my grandchildren, Melanie, Guy, April, Ian,
Taniee, Kalem, Kai and Kelly.

Acknowledgements

Thanks first and foremost to my guide and very dear friend White Feather, without whom there would be no book.

To dear Ruth and Leslie Bone, both now in Spirit, who recognised something in me I could not see for myself and set me on my Spiritual path. My grateful thanks.

To Denyse Pettle (now in Spirit), a lovely lady and a very good medium who gave me confidence to look forward and put my gift to good use for Spirit.

To Kerys Laughing Bear, a Celtic/Amerindian Crow, a teacher, reader and healer in Native American Spiritualism, who has answered many questions concerning my guide, White Feather, and where my true path lies.

To Merlynne White Bear, my tutor for shamanic healing, for her understanding and encouragement and for being on the same wavelength as myself.

Last but not least, thanks to my husband Vic for his patience, understanding and support.

Foreword

The Spirit World is all around us, as real as our own, and there are rare individuals who are permitted to raise a little, the veil that divides us from a higher truth. When, as in this case, these experiences are shared, every reader gains. This book is one that helps us understand a little more, the complex and strange ways of creation.

Mark Sykes
Athena Press

About the Author

My name is Geraldine Pengelly and I was born in Rotherhithe, London in 1934. During the war I was evacuated to Wiltshire, returning home just after VE day. I have had many ups and downs during my life. My first marriage ended after fifteen years and three children (plus one miscarriage) in 1969. In 1971 I met my present husband, Victor, and we decided to move to Basingstoke to start a new life.

In the mid seventies, I lost both my parents. This then brought about my first encounter with Spiritualism. I was invited to attend a Spiritual Healer, to help me with my bereavement, and subsequently joined a circle at the home of the healer. Whilst attending the weekly circle, I was encouraged to develop my clairvoyance and clairaudience.

Such is life, after a few years other matters overtook my life and Spiritualism was put on the backburner.

We moved to Andover, Hampshire, in 1992 and at that time my husband had been suffering panic attacks and had been treated by our doctor. After we had been in our new home a while, my husband got worse. I do not know who it came from, but I heard a voice telling me to find a healer, which I did.

Since that first visit to the healer for my husband's panic attacks, I have been involved with all matters Spiritual. My thirst for more and more knowledge led me to discovering people like John Edward, and reading his books, learning about the process and listening to his tapes.

About three years ago my interest in wanting to know more about my guide and the 'closeness' I felt towards him led me to an Amerindian Crow by the name of Kerys Laughing Bear. Kerys lived in Devon and I found him whilst reading a mind, body and Spirit magazine. Kerys and I have become very good friends and, strange as it may seem to you, we have never met in person. We have written letters to each other, had numerous calls and exchanged gifts. Kerys has made me a medicine shield, a drum and a rattle. I made him a couple of blankets (I crotchet squares and sew them together) for him to use when he goes walkabout. At present, Kerys is in New Zealand following a calling he had to go and work there.

My Spiritual path then led me to Shamanic work. After completing my studies, I received my diploma as a shamanic practitioner, and was given the name 'Red Fox' Medicine Woman. This work has brought me even closer to my guide, White Feather, and makes me feel that in my previous, or one of my previous lives, we were in fact related. I hope, in time, to discover that this is true.

Introduction

My purpose in writing this book is to share with you my travels with my guide, White Feather, and the many things he taught me. For those of you who are already involved and working for Spirit I hope this book will uplift you and perhaps answer any questions that you have thought about from time to time. To those who are eager to learn more about Spirit, perhaps this will be a starting point for you and give you an insight into the wonderful things that happen when you open your heart to Spirit. Always remember that although our physical bodies die, our Spirit lives on eternally.

Perhaps some of you have picked up this book out of curiosity, not really believing in an afterlife. To these people I say, read on and you never know, you may become believers. Someone once said that life after death is rubbish and that when you're dead you're dead. How sad. I feel that that person is in for one heck of a shock when it is their time to leave this earth…

Contents

Introduction to Spiritualism

My interest in Spiritualism started somewhat late in life, when I was forty-two. The year was 1976 and both my parents had passed away, Mum in February 1974 and Dad in May 1976. I had three children, was working full-time and was living a normal life. When my parents died I felt completely devastated. Anyone who has lost one or both parents will know the feeling well. I was also very angry because they went so early: they were only in their early sixties.

Around that time I met a very nice lady who worked for the same company as I did, although didn't work alongside me. Her name was Ruth. She was very kind to me, encouraging me to talk about my bereavement and offering to introduce me to her husband, Leslie, who was a Spiritual healer. She said she felt I needed some healing. For some reason I didn't doubt her or feel any fear. I did not even question what 'Spiritual healing' was: I just went to see him.

My healing sessions with both Ruth and Leslie gave me such wonderful feelings of utter peace and tranquillity that I felt a little sad as each one came to an end. But I looked forward to the following week when I would again visit and once again find myself with this feeling.

As I grew stronger and left my despair behind, I began sitting in the weekly circle meetings with Ruth and Leslie. My husband was invited to sit also. Our weekly meetings went from strength to strength and I began to be aware of pictures in my mind. I also started to hear voices: they were a little muffled at first but became clearer as time went on. During our circle times Leslie encouraged me, helping me to develop my clairvoyance and clairaudience, and slowly I realised that I was becoming more and more aware of Spirit. This time was also my first introduction to White Feather and trance mediumship.

Unfortunately, such as life is, over the next few years circumstances prevented me from developing further and all thoughts connected to Spirit were pushed to one side. My full-time employment ended with redundancy, we moved out of the area and life took a different turn. When we had been living in our new abode for a while, my husband suddenly started having panic attacks. I heard a voice in my head telling me to find a healer, and after scanning the local newspaper discovered a house where healing was given one evening a week. A visit was arranged for my husband to receive healing and I accompanied him. When we arrived we were shown into a very large room being used for healing at one end and as a waiting area at the other. The lady who came forward to greet us introduced herself and then asked if I was a medium. I was quite surprised by her question and must have shown my feelings by the look on my face. She then said that as soon as I walked into the room they all felt a surge of energy. So, I thought, this is what I am: a powerhouse, an instrument of energy. During the following weeks whilst my husband received healing, I joined the group's weekly circle and went to church on Sunday evenings. At one of the church gatherings, a medium who had been giving readings to the congregation suddenly 'dried up'. Before I understood what was happening, I felt a push in the middle of my back and my hand shot up in the air. I was asking for permission to sit in the front row facing the medium. Permission given, I changed seats and within seconds the medium was back on course, giving messages from Spirit to friends and families that were there. At the end of the meeting I left the hall feeling quite drained. Once again the thought came. 'Power-pack energy': is this what I am needed for?

After about six weeks of attending the circle, I began to feel restless and could not settle. One particular evening I felt really uncomfortable. I closed my eyes and prayed for help. I asked for guidance and help to settle this feeling I had of wanting to just get up out of my chair and go. I was aware of an old gentleman with a long white beard standing in front of me. He was shaking his head at me and saying over and over again, 'No, no, no.' I knew that he had come from Spirit, for no one else saw him, only I. Once again, I felt unsure of what was required of me by Spirit. Spirit wanted me for something, but what?

That was September 2001.

In March 2002 I asked my husband if he could buy the *Psychic News* from the newsagents. I don't know why: I only know that I had to get this paper. The newsagent did not stock the paper but arranged to get it. We started to receive the paper on a weekly basis and each week I read it from cover to cover. In May a small advert appeared concerning a psychic fair that was being held in the next county the following month. I felt a strong urge to attend this event and after my husband and I talked about it, we both decided to go. It was here that we met Denyse Pettle.

The psychic fair was held in a lovely cottage garden; it was quite large, with four booths staggered around the perimeter. Two of the booths were being used for readings, one was for a psychic artist and aura readings, and one had various items for sale such as candles and pouches for stones. Our hosts, Denise and Laurie, greeted us with cups of tea and coffee and made us feel very welcome. Denise is an artist and has painted some beautiful pictures, all inspired by Spirit. Her husband Laurie is a trance medium and healer. There were quite a few people there and the atmosphere was one of tranquillity and happiness. Even the weather was on its best behaviour, with the sun shining; it was a beautiful day.

My husband went into one of the booths for a reading whilst I, after finishing my coffee, wandered over to a group of people who were just sitting talking. One of the women in the group had just received some healing and we began talking. She told me she was a healer but had been down a bit lately and had come for a 'booster' healing session. She asked me what I did. I said, 'I'm not sure but I think I am some sort of energy box.' She laughed and said, 'Perhaps Spirit sent you to sit next to me to give me some energy.' We chatted for a while and then my husband returned from his reading. He told me to go to the booth for my reading. This was my first contact with Denyse Pettle.

I shook hands with Denyse and she asked, 'What are you doing with all the information you've been receiving from Spirit?' She mentioned a few things I knew but hadn't spoken about to anyone and told me I should be telling people, not keeping them to myself. Denyse then asked me to choose one of three hoops of coloured ribbons she held on her arm. I chose the smallest hoop.

She then asked me to close my eyes and pick three ribbons from the hoop that she had placed in front of me. This I did. Then Denyse asked me to open my eyes. She looked at me for a while and then said, 'It is the first time that this has happened in all the years I have been working as a medium. You chose the same hoop and exactly the same colour ribbons as your husband did. You are ready now to work for Spirit: always work with love and have faith in Spirit. Your shopping basket will never be empty and the choice of how you work will be yours: it could be one-to-one, by rostrum or by written work.' She asked me if I felt excited by all that was coming my way. In one way I did, and in another I must admit to feeling a little apprehensive about speaking to people even on a one-to-one basis about messages I was hearing in my head. Suppose they laughed at me? How would I react? When my reading with Denyse came to a close, she asked me for a hug, saying, 'Let me have some of that energy.'

We left the fair, and as we walked to the car discussing our readings, my husband and I felt that we had both been given a boost by what we had heard. We had plenty to think about as we drove home.

Denyse had told us that we should now be thinking of forming our own circle and had said to my husband that he should begin a course in hypnotherapy, for this was his way forward. Once he had gained his diploma he could begin his healing clinic. This would be his daily work in his forthcoming retirement and would keep him busy. The other prediction he was given was that his family would grow. As you can imagine, we had so much to think about that we talked of nothing else for days.

A few weeks after our readings, whilst looking

through the *Psychic News*, my attention was drawn to an advertisement by a psychic artist by the name of Lynn Rose. For the princely sum of twenty pounds she would paint a portrait of your guide and also give you the message she received whilst painting the picture. I duly sent my money and wrote a few lines about myself and asked for a portrait of my guide. Three weeks later the picture arrived and when I opened the envelope I just cried. I was looking at a Native American Indian with the kindest face I had ever seen. His eyes were the most striking feature; they seemed to look right through me. I just sat holding the picture and looking at him, feeling completely happy and content. It seemed that I was looking at a very old friend, one I had not seen for years. *I knew then that this gentleman was special.*

The message that came with the drawing read as follows:

> Information received with drawing of guide for Geraldine Pengelly. Dated 3 August 2002:
>
> *My dear child, I am so pleased to be able to show myself to you in this way. You and I have been together for a long time now and are no strangers. It matters not that you have not seen me. You have felt the energy that surrounds me, and that is all that matters. I am of course only one of those who walk at your side and indeed this is an honour. You have many gifts, child, although you have yet to realise them fully. You have been through many experiences on the way to the present and all your experiences have enabled you to gain wisdom that could not have been gained in any other way. Life is for learning, child, not for material gain. For it matters not how much you have when you pass to Spirit as it mattered not what you had when you entered this world. What matters is what you gain from life in the*

Spiritual sense. Life is one long learning experience, and understanding this small fact takes many all of their lives. You, child, are understanding now and this is good, for you have your true work to do. You have the ability to communicate with the Spirit and you will help many people along your way. We will assist you and guard and guide you, child. You will learn that there are many ways of communication between the two worlds, as indeed there are in your world. Learn to feel and sense the energies around you, use your intuition to guide you and always work with the power of love and all will be as it should be. Sit in the quiet with my image and we will learn to communicate together. Take note of the thoughts and feelings as they come to mind, child, and you will indeed learn about the art of communicating with the Spirit. Remember that the love and the light of the great and powerful Spirit are always with you and part of you.

I read and re-read this message many times: it was as if I could not hear his words enough. I suppose it was something like being really, really hungry and suddenly a plate of food arrives in front of you and you just cannot stop eating. This lovely soul was my guide and mentor. His name was White Feather. Now I knew my journey had truly begun, a journey of discovery about Spirit, the future and myself.

New Beginnings

My first sitting with White Feather began on Wednesday, 7 August 2002 and, as he instructed, I have kept a daily log of everything that has happened since that date. I will now write from this logbook (to date I have filled four A5 books).

Wednesday, 7 August 2002

This is my first sitting with White Feather. At 7 a.m. I was told to rise and to sit with his image. His actual words to me were, 'Come, child, we are alone and we can talk. I will tell you a little about myself; look at me and all will become clear.' White Feather told me that his Spiritual home was on the third plane but for my lifetime he would be with me. I asked about his life on earth, eager to know everything there was to know about this dear soul. His earth life was mainly spent in Dakota. He had a wife and three fine sons. He was not a chief but did sit on many types of council in his village. He gave me a date 1864. White Feather told me I need to drink more water. I am to set aside a little time each day to talk with him and he will guide me. Each day we will take a new step together. His promise to me is that my heart will become lighter and my vision clearer. He will always be there to protect me and keep me safe from any darkness that threatens. White Feather tells me that I have a very strong power but I need to let go of whatever is holding me back from committing myself fully to Spirit. Each time we speak I will get a little stronger. To begin with we will spend just a short time speaking and extend this in the fullness of time. At first I shall feel a little tired after each session, but he assures me that all tiredness will fade as we progress along the Spiritual path. White Feather tells me that we will make many journeys together: there are many places he wishes to show me. His final words to me were: 'I will not leave you, child. Your heart is strong. Listen to your heart.

'Yeha Noha.'

(*This signing off 'Yeha Noha' is given at the end of each session and after communication. I found out about a year later when I started to communicate with Kerys Laughing Bear that it is a 'go thee well' type of expression.*)

As you can imagine, my brain was working overtime after this. I duly read his words again and again. He had not told me a lot about himself, and the date of 1864 could have been his date of birth or a date significant to him alone. This was something that Kerys Laughing Bear told me about later. This was the year he left the earth plain.

Thursday, 8 August

We started our lesson a bit late today; White Feather understands that daily tasks have to be done first. Today White Feather gave me my Spiritual name, Sehywha; this is pronounced 'Seeway'.

'Our talk today, child, concerns the feelings you have concerning your path ahead. I will try to speak so that you may understand. Many people feel insecure, not having any awareness save of themselves. Many times in the past you have been hurt by words. Words, my child, can be as sharp as arrowheads and, for someone like yourself, more painful. Because of this you are afraid to speak, for what you may say may cause pain to others. It is a sad way of the world, my child, that many people say and do things that cause others pain. Here in Spirit pain such as this is not known. Many lessons have been learnt by souls that come to Spirit; they see what their words and deeds have done and are filled with remorse, and thus their first lesson is learned. The time will come when you will have to speak to many people and say exactly what you feel. We have also pondered your reluctance to say what you feel. You must have faith in what you do, child. You have a fear of being made to look foolish if your words do not carry the correct information. In Spirit we do not speak, for there is no need; the thought of one is passed to another, thus the receiver of the thought takes the purity of what is being said. So shall it be with you, child; you will hear the thought and the tongue will then speak the thought. If the person does not accept the words, then look to find the inner face. Then, my child, you will see the truth and know that your words are true. Then we must pray for them to feel the warmth of the Spirit.

'Now, Sehywha, we will end our teachings for this time. Do not be afraid to use your knowledge. It is a precious gift. Feel the love from Spirit that surrounds you. Learning is a joy, but too much at one time can confuse one. When you are hot feel the cool waters of the mountain stream passing over you.

'Yeha Noha.'

(I feel quite drained. Going to have a long sit-down and digest all this information.)

I did not question what I had been told by White Feather. His words were softly spoken and his voice gave me a feeling of utter peace. As with the visits to Ruth and Leslie Bone, I felt the need for more knowledge of Spirit. I started to buy books on everything connected to Spiritualism and read all I possibly could. I also decided (or Spirit did) that I should keep a diary, noting everything White Feather spoke about and any dreams that I had. As you will see as we progress further through this book, I do not believe in coincidence. Everything happens for a reason. The answer may not come straight away as to why this or that happens, but it will come, I can assure you.

In my search to gain more Spiritual knowledge I began to watch programmes on TV like *Crossing Over* with John Edward and *Sixth Sense* with Colin Fry. I also watched Derek Acorah whenever he appeared in a Spiritual programme. The more I listened to what was being said the more I wanted to hear. At the end of one of his programmes, John Edward mentioned his meditation tapes. A few days later whilst browsing through a magazine I came across a section on Body, Mind and Soul, and there were the meditation tapes John had spoken about. The thought came to purchase these, as they would help me to relax more and get closer to Spirit. The tapes arrived and I began listening to them. I decided to do as the first tape instructed, and to set a little time aside each day to meditate and just listen to John's voice. After a while I realised that a whole new world had opened up to me. The more I meditated the brighter the picture got and the clearer the thought came. Meditation and prayers are very important to those who wish to hear the inner voice. White Feather has told me to always work with love and prayer and all will be as it should be. It is very hard to explain on paper the feelings that you have after spending time in meditation, but I will try.

The first noticeable thing is how relaxed you feel: one part of you feels full of energy, ready for anything; the other part feels warm and cosy, leaving you with an inner glow. By sitting quietly, even just for fifteen minutes or so, you feel a sharpening of your senses: hearing, feeling and sight. Meditation is a good discipline and if done on a regular basis, say every morning upon waking, can improve your day by giving you a feeling of well-being and contentment. Meditation has given me the ability to calmly take each day as it comes and to be prepared for anything the world might choose to throw at me. It has enabled me to give thanks at the end of each day for the good things as well as the bad things, for even the bad things are experiences and teach a lesson.

My next sitting with White Feather was on the following Monday morning. For some reason we do not have lessons at the weekends: I think this is because there is too much coming and going, visitors etc., but here again I do not question.

Monday, 12 August

We began today's communication with music. I was told to close my ears to the outside world and to listen. I heard music: at first it was very soft, and then it began to get louder. It was very calming, a mixture of soft bells and pipes (similar to panpipes) together with a drum. White Feather told me to breathe in time with the drumbeat and to have no fear, for no harm would come to me. He said just to let myself go and trust him. The music was very plaintive and moving, and suddenly I began to see pictures. I was somewhere in the mountains, which were snow-capped; the sun was shining and the sky was very blue.

I seemed to be on some kind of turntable that turned very slowly, enabling me to take in the beauty of the place. It was truly breathtaking. The music grew louder until it echoed all around me. White Feather spoke: 'Now you have seen one of the many places we shall visit, Sehywha. Whenever you cannot sit in the quiet and communicate with me you will have this memory to uplift you. There will be others, but for now this is the place you must go to when you need to feel close to Spirit. Although we will not speak, you will feel my presence and feel refreshed. My child, I know that I do not have to tell you to clear your mind before you begin the journey. This is so that you will feel the full benefit of this wondrous place. Many thoughts fill your mind; do not concern yourself with matters of the world you cannot control. We know of your concerns over the lost children (*this last comment was in relation to two little girls who had gone missing from their homes*) and that you stretch your mind to find answers. Do not, for this will drain your energy: instead include them in your prayers. One prayer sent to Spirit will help those who search for the truth, enabling them to find the answers.'

White Feather continued with: 'This one is truly honoured that his image has a permanent place in your lodge. Please to give my thoughts of gratitude to the one who made this possible. We shall speak again soon, child.

'Yeha Noha.'

White Feather's thanks were duly passed to my husband, who has framed his portrait and hung it on the wall across from my armchair, so that he is facing me.

As I went though my day, my thoughts kept straying to what had transpired earlier with White Feather: the image of the lake like a mirror reflecting the snow-capped mountains; the beautiful blue of the sky and the simultaneous sense I felt of calmness and exhilaration. I knew that White Feather had told me that this was just one of the many places we would visit, and wondered what the others would be like; surely nothing could compare with this beautiful place. I eagerly looked forward to tomorrow.

Tuesday, 13 August

My lesson today, White Feather tells me, is touch. White Feather tells me to sit with my hands resting on my thighs, palms facing upward. White Feather said, 'This will be a new experience for you, child, so do not be afraid. Nothing ugly or harmful will be given. We will try to distinguish different shapes, materials and perhaps colour. When we have completed this exercise you will describe what you have held in your hands.'

I was given three items. Two I got right, but the third one fooled me completely. The first felt like a stone. I saw a flash of colour (blue); the size roughly was one inch in length and half an inch deep. I was then shown the object and given the words 'Well done.'

It was a coloured stone of a very deep blue. This is a healing stone. The second object felt like a flower petal, very soft and delicate. I felt the colour white and then the impression changed to pink. The item, when it was shown to me, proved to be a white rose petal, and quite a large one at that: this rose is love. White Feather said I must feel and see the colour and always go with the first impression. The last item was about the size of my palm, with pieces cut out or missing. I decided that it must be an artist's palette. Wrong! When I saw it, I discovered it was a large piece of a jigsaw puzzle. I was told, 'This is one small part of the whole picture. Make sure you have all the pieces and that they fit together before speaking of what you see.' White Feather told me that there would be times when the images I could see would change from the first impression I got. 'Always go with the first impression,' he said. This would be the clairvoyance part of my learning.

I asked White Feather if it would possible for me to go through the small fanlight window in the bedroom. This was something that had happened to me a while ago. One minute I was in bed, the next I had passed through the fanlight and was standing on the lawn looking at the outside of my home. I was not sure if it was a dream or if it had really happened. The answer he gave me was, 'All things are possible, my child. Believe in yourself.'

White Feather told me to rest well today once my chores are done. I will need all my energy for the next step. I asked if I could continue with my meditation tapes as I find them helpful and was told to do so.

Wednesday, 14 August

Early start today. I heard White Feather asking me to sit after my meditation. I heard the music again as before and after a while felt myself floating. White Feather told me we were returning to the mountains and the lake of tranquillity that we had visited before. This time I found myself walking across lush green grass towards the beautiful lake. The water was almost turquoise in colour and very still; the mountains reflected on the surface of the lake. All was still and calm. There was a log-type bench by the side of the lake and I was told to sit and to look into the water and to feel the calmness of the lake, to drink in the absolute peace and beauty of the place, and to fill the whole of my being with the feelings I was being given. I do not know how long I sat. I felt very relaxed: the water was almost hypnotic and made me feel very sleepy. White Feather spoke to me softly: 'Turn yourself around, child, and look beneath the trees.' I did as he asked and could not believe my eyes: there was my mother holding her arms out to me. I leapt to my feet and ran as fast as I could towards her. We hugged each other. Mum was smiling and I was crying with sheer joy. We did not speak: there was no need. I understood her thoughts as she did mine. There were children hiding beneath her skirt. This game, hide and seek, is still a favourite. They also enjoy swimming and singing. My mother looked radiant and so happy.

Standing to Mum's right was a tall young man with very blue eyes; he reminded me of my father, but younger. I did not think that they would show me my mother as I had last seen her, minus ten or fifteen years – say when she was in her early forties – and then show me Dad at twenty-five or twenty-seven. My mother had a cheeky look in her eyes and she asked if I knew who this young man was. I looked at him: he was smiling at me and seemed so familiar but at the same time a stranger (it is very hard to express the feelings going through me at this point). I kept looking at them and then I just knew. He was my son, the first child that I had miscarried just before my eldest daughter was born. My emotions were just too much for me. Once again I was crying as I hugged my son.

Then I was sitting back on the log and looking into the lake again. White Feather told me it was time to return. 'There will be other times, child, many other times.' I told him that I did not want to leave this place, but he said I must. These visits are both uplifting and sad. I suppose it is not really sadness, but something similar to coming to the end of a really great holiday when it is over and time to go home.

I'm back on terra firma. White Feather's voice came from a little way off. 'What are you feeling now, child?' he asked. I told him that I felt great. He said, 'Good, that is what we wanted to hear. Our next journey will be longer. There are many more beautiful places we wish you to see. As always, my child, rest well. We are here. You have truly earned the contentment in your heart.

'Yeha Noha.'

Thursday, 15 August

I had been waiting about ten minutes after having showered and washed my hair for White Feather to speak (I could feel his presence even though he hadn't yet spoken), when I began to hear the music I have begun to associate with him. After this, he spoke: 'We are going on a journey, child: this time, it will be one of observation. Be sure to mind everything you see, child, that way the writing will flow easily. Close your eyes, listen to the music and breathe in step with the drum. As you see, child, this one wears his war bonnet to show how fine the colours are and, if we can be forgiven for this one time, to show how magnificent this one looked long ago.

Keep this in mind, child, for this is how you will see me when you look.' (*I took this to mean that there is a picture or photograph of him somewhere, perhaps in a book – this will be a validation for me.*)

The place we are in is like being inside one minute and outside the next. There is a large building to my left: it is huge and supported by white pillars. We climb the steps; these are in a pink and black patterned marble mosaic. We do not go in: we just look in through the doorway. It is quite cool, quiet and peaceful. White Feather tells me that this is the hall for new arrivals: that is, for those Spirits who have crossed over and need to rest for a period of time.

There are rows upon rows of hammocks, swaying very slightly as if in a soft breeze. There are also people who look like doctors moving around, all dressed in white. We leave this place, and at the foot of the marble steps we turn right and see a huge lake. From the centre of the lake rise seven fountains: each one is a different colour. Just like a rainbow, the colours fall into a semicircle before going back into the water. On the far side of the lake there is another large building. White Feather tells me that this is one of many that teach. It would seem that we still have things to learn when we cross over into Spirit.

The scenery changes from open space, lush lawns and flowerbeds to woodland. The surface is soft and springy underfoot. Coming out of the woodland is a wide expanse of water and in the distance many more buildings. These, I am told, are for art and creativity. I cannot see the sun but the sky is blue and it feels very warm. We pass many faces. They do not speak: they only smile. Even though I am surrounded with people, I feel alone.

White Feather tells me that this is because I am still a child of Mother Earth. When I finally make my transition, when it is my time, I will understand these feelings.

We have come to what looks like a crossroads. There are many paths leading out in different directions. Each pathway seems to have different coloured steppingstones. I am told to choose a path, and the one I choose is the blue path. That, I am told, is the path that is associated with healing. I will learn more about this in the near future. White Feather tells me we must return and says: 'You have seen only a very small part of our Spiritual plane: there is much, much more to experience.' I am told that each time we complete a communication or journey I will feel stronger, learn from the information I have been given and become wiser. 'Rest well, my child. We are here.

'Yeha Noha.'

This has got to be the biggest thing to have happened to me yet: how can I possibly resume my mundane chores after this? I sat for quite a long time after I had written my journal, re-living every part of what I had seen over and over again. The other thing that came into my head was, who would believe what I had seen?

Monday, 19 August

Today we did not travel. White Feather told me to sit quietly to receive healing. The music began, very softly (again similar to panpipes). I began to feel someone's hands on the top of my head. The hands did not rest on my head but just above it. I could feel the warmth of these hands as they moved from the top of my head down to my shoulders, chest and back, continuing down to my hips and legs and finally to my feet. I felt very peaceful and calm. At the end of the healing session I heard White Feather speak: 'Very soon, my child, people will arrive at your door, some in need of healing, some looking for answers to questions concerning their problems or matters of the future. Each day, child, we will sit before we talk so that we can give you energy for your healing work. This will gradually build: some will be for yourself and some for those who come.

'Another old friend will be with you at healing times, child. (*No name was given but I immediately got the impression of Leslie Bone.*) From these healing times will come questions. Thus will begin your mediumship. Do not be afraid, child: we shall be here to guide you. Prayers filled with love for those who come for healing and all those in Spirit who assist at these times should be offered to the Great Spirit. You will know from our talks, child, that it is important to push away impure thoughts. Let your being be filled with love. Love and kindness given to one will bring back the same, threefold. Rest well, my child.

'Yeha Noha.'

In the next sitting we shall be speaking of two photographs. One, which was taken at my youngest son's house, is a photograph of my grandson, Kai, sitting on his toy tractor in front of the fireplace. The other is a photo of some trees at the back of our home. The camera went off accidentally in this photo, or at least that is what we thought until the film was developed! The first photo of Kai was taken by Polaroid, and although it is still visible at the time of writing, I do not know how long it will last before it fades away.

I had spoken to my mother a few days earlier, asking if she was still around as I had not heard from her for a while. The answer came back: 'Of course I am. Look in the recent photo you took.' I searched through all the recent photographs without success and then I remembered that my husband had taken his Polaroid camera when we visited Mark's the weekend previously. I eventually found them on our mantelpiece, tucked away behind an ornament. Well, my friends, to say I was absolutely amazed would be an understatement, for there, sitting just behind Kai's right shoulder, was the image of my mother in an oval-shaped frame of light. I was so excited I rang both my husband at work and my son Mark. Mark said, 'Tell Nanny not to disappear before the weekend; we are coming to see her.' When we all gathered on the following Sunday we studied the photograph and decided that there was no way it could have been a reflection of anything in the room, not from the angle it was taken. This was, as far as I am concerned, a proof that Mum is still around us. I thanked Mum for this gift and heard her voice telling me that she would be with Mark for a little while to give him a 'boost' (Mark had recently come out of hospital after an operation and was feeling a little wobbly).

The second photograph, of the trees at the back of our house, was the last from a reel of film we had taken while on holiday earlier in the year. When the photographs came back from the developer's and we looked at them, I nearly fell off my chair! In the very last photo, perched in the trees inside what looked like a TV screen, was my father's face. I just could not believe what I was seeing. Although I had not heard from my father for quite a while, he was always in my thoughts. Given the kind of joker he was, I felt that this was his funny way of letting me know that Mum was not the only one who could send us a picture from Spirit. Thanks, Dad, you made my day!

Tuesday, 20 August

As yesterday, healing for the first part of the sitting. Soft music and the feeling of healing hands. After the healing, White Feather spoke very softly, asking me to speak the questions in my head. I asked him about the photographs and the strong feelings I had. The answer came back: 'Believe in what you see, child.' I told him that my husband's vision of the photograph of my father was quite different to mine. He had seen my mother quite clearly but he could not see the image of my father as I had. The answer came: 'Everyone sees what they wish to see, child. Sometimes the person looking looks too deep. There is no need to look long and hard, for this distorts the soul's eye and can cause images to change from one thing to another. Have faith in what you see. As we have said before, child, clear your mind of all other matters, and fill your thoughts of the quiet times we spend together. Only in the quiet will you be able to gain knowledge and see further than before.'

I asked White Feather about my husband's development, because since our meeting with Denyse I feel that I am galloping away with my awareness and I suppose I expected my husband to do the same. The answer from White Feather was, 'This one is here to guide you, child, on your journey, and as such can only say to you that the words must come from what you see. Encouragement should be given to spending time together in the quiet, to clear all thoughts of everything except Spirit. The desire to speak with and hear Spirit will be his ultimate goal. Perhaps writing in the quiet, as you do. Soon your knowledge of what you have seen and heard will be tested. Have no fear, child; we are with you and will guide you through the mists of disbelief. You grow stronger each day and soon there will come a time when you will be able to shrug away taunts and denials. Because of what you have seen and heard you think others must be aware also. Not everyone has the patience to sit in the quiet and listen. There are too many who say, "Show me and I will believe." Many examples of this can be shown but you do not need to know, child, for you already have the knowledge.

'Enough words for this time, child: too many thoughts cause confusion. Think now only of the images this one gives you and of that special place (*the lake*). Go there, child, when you seek peace. Rest well.

'Yeha Noha.'

Although it has only been three weeks since my first sitting with White Feather, it seems that I have known him all my life. I find myself eagerly waiting each day to hear his voice and, on the occasions that we travel, to see him. I never question what he tells me because I know that he speaks only the truth. I trust him implicitly and find myself wanting to know more about him. White Feather is reluctant to tell me more about himself: he just tells me that he is here to teach and guide me and that this is sufficient for now. The other thing I have noticed is that since we began these daily sittings I feel stronger in myself. I seem to sail through my daily tasks with very little effort. For example, a huge pile of ironing looks daunting but, as soon as I start, it seems I am ironing the last item. Each task I do seems to take less time than it did before and this is, I know, because I am being given help from Spirit.

The next sitting really blew my mind. I shall let the following speak for itself.

Wednesday, 21 August

We began today with a lesson in observation. White Feather said, 'Your prayers for the lost children have been many, my child. They are now being looked after by gentle souls who will wipe away all bad memories. But you knew they were with Spirit, for did you not see them, child? Think of the time you met and spoke with your earth mother. They showed you their faces. Remember, child, the piece of jigsaw: see the whole image, not just a part. We know that the excitement of seeing a loved one long gone blinded your vision to other things being shown to you. (*These were the two missing girls who had concerned me and, after White Feather's comments on seeing the whole picture, I remembered these were the two little faces I had seen peeping out from behind my mother's skirt – the sitting on Wednesday, 14 August.*) This learning will stay with you and remind you in the future to look at the whole image before you.'

White Feather told me to listen to the music and to breathe in rhythm to the beat of the drum. He tells me we are going on a journey to somewhere new: 'Your liking for water, be it of the sea or of the river, shows that it is the right place for you. You can identify with the meaning of water: life!'

I listened to the music I could hear being played and felt myself beginning to float upwards. After a short time I was told to open my eyes and to look around me.

I was by a river, which flowed over stones and was shallow enough that I could see the bottom. On the bank of the river was a fallen tree. I was told to sit and look into the water. What happened next is most extraordinary. I felt something soft against my legs. I looked and could not believe what I saw. A very large lion was sitting, leaning against my legs. I felt a moment of sheer panic. White Feather said, 'Do not be afraid, child, for no harm will come to you. Look into his eyes and see the kindness and love in his soul. Touch him: feel his strength.' Encouraged by White Feather's words, I did as he asked. I looked into the lion's huge amber eyes and felt the warmth of his love. Then I touched him. I stroked his mane, then his face. White Feather said, 'Feel his strength, child, let this strength flow into you.' The lion put one of his paws on my lap. It did not feel heavy. I stroked the lion's paw and realised I felt no fear at all.

'How do you feel, child?' I told him that I felt very happy and was not afraid of the lion any more. His answer was, 'Good. Take the memory of the lion and keep it within you, child. He will give you the strength you will need for the times ahead.' I felt the lion softly lick my hand and although his tongue was very rough he did not hurt me. Once again I was told to look into the water, and then I was back in my chair in familiar surroundings. White Feather: 'Rest well, child, we shall speak again soon.

'Yeha Noha.'

Once again words cannot describe my feelings – fantastic, wonderful, amazing being just a few. When I think about all these experiences I am being given I feel very humble and ask myself what I have done to deserve such an honour. White Feather tells me that it is just the beginning and that there is much more to come. I just hope that my poor old heart can stand the excitement it is receiving. I am now in my sixty-eighth year and wish that this could have happened much earlier in my life. When I asked White Feather why it hadn't, he told me that it was because I was not ready for all this twenty or so years ago. It is because I had to experience life with all its ups and downs. Now it seems I am ready. When I look back, I suppose my life has been a bit of a big dipper, but no more than what other people have to suffer. There are plenty more who have experienced many more trials and tribulations than I, during their time on this earth. I am one of the lucky ones. Spirit stepped in when I needed it most.

For this next sitting I need to set the scene, as it were, so that the message given by White Feather is understandable. Last evening my husband and myself were sitting at the kitchen table, talking. Suddenly I became aware of a young man in uniform standing in the doorway between the kitchen and the lounge. He was wearing a red tunic with big brass buttons and had a white helmet on his head. He disappeared and then a few seconds later appeared again. My husband, unaware of what I was seeing, had apparently asked me a question. When I did not answer him, he shouted at me. (Something like, 'Hello, anyone in?') I shook myself and explained what I was seeing and that I had not realised he had been speaking to me. The following will speak for itself.

Thursday, 22 August

I was asked to sit earlier today. In fact I was woken up at 6.45 a.m. by White Feather calling me. I was told to sit with pen and paper. I felt a surge of energy as White Feather came through.

'Please to sit, child. These words must be written as we speak. This way the words come straight from this one to the paper.' I did as he asked, but had to ask him to slow down so that I could keep up with his words. This message is for my husband.

'My son, you do not yet know me: you only know of what Sehywha has spoken. We are here to guide this child on her Spiritual path, one that you, too, may share. There are many things you have yet to learn; all will become clear in the fullness of time.

'Sehywha has chosen to follow the path that has been laid down for her. She will now become more aware than before: images will be shown at times other than when she sits in the quiet. She will need all her strength to work with and accept what she is being shown. Sehywha makes good progress, as we knew she would. She will not leave you behind, my son. Because her knowledge of Spirit is greater than yours at the present time, she will in turn guide you in your development. You are her husband, the love of her life. You must also be her friend. Please be patient. If she does not answer you directly it is because she is being shown images that will mean and prove to be important at some later stage. We ask you not to raise your voice at these times. Sehywha is a sensitive soul: more so than others who are not aware of the Spirit. There is also a path for you to follow, my son: one that will be both happy and fulfilling. Your path and Sehywha's will bring much happiness and contentment to those who seek your help. This one's words are spoken: please know that they come with love and are meant to make you aware of things that may distract Sehywha's awareness, holding back her progress as well as yours.'

I sat for about ten minutes after White Feather had finished speaking, thinking about what he had said and how my husband would react to his words. I sat a little longer wondering if White Feather would speak again, but I felt he had gone as there was no energy left. For myself I felt quite drained; perhaps he had gone to recharge his batteries. I was about to close my notebook when White Feather came back: 'The answer to your question, child, is…' I was then shown the image of the soldier again, the one I saw last evening in a red jacket and white helmet, and I was given the words 'Rorke's Drift, my rifle jammed, too much smoke, can't see a bloody thing.' (Not sure if the spelling of 'Rorke's Drift' is correct.) Nothing else was given, White Feather has gone; he usually says 'Yeha Noha', but he has not done so today.

I found myself wondering about this soldier and the reason for his appearance. As I get more and more into anything to do with Spirit I find that at some stage down the line I will be able to identify what I am shown and the reason. So I put it to the back of my mind, what I call 'filing under miscellaneous', until I need to bring it out again.

Later that day, just after I had finished watching John Edward, I heard White Feather calling me. 'Come, child, we go to the lake to talk of many things.' I switched off the TV and sat in my chair and waited. I heard White Feather telling me to relax and listen to the music that was being played. At first it played very softly, and then it seemed to be all around me. I began to float. It felt like I was floating on a cushion of warm air: it was very comfortable and reassuring.

We are by the lake, which is very still. The tall trees, which look like pine trees, are reflected in the water. White Feather is sitting on the grass and motions to me to sit with him. After I sit he asks me if I am comfortable. I tell him I am.

I look around me: all is very peaceful and still. In front of White Feather is a small fire of wood. He picks up a piece of what looks like a small bunch of heather and holds it in the fire until it starts to burn. He lifts it to his mouth and blows it until the flame goes out and it is just smouldering. He holds this in front of him, then waves it towards his body. He uses his other hand to pull the smoke from it towards his body in a circular movement. He passes the bunch to me and says, 'Do as I did, child.' The smoke smells like pine needles and another smell I cannot quite recognise. Later during my many lessons I learnt that this aroma was cedar and that the exercise we were doing was called 'smudging'. Before any ceremonies or any decision making, the Native American Indians would smudge themselves to take any unwanted energies away, so the smoke acted as a purifier. White Feather tells me that I should do this before my sittings. The smoke will take away any potentially negative energy.

I find White Feather's presence very comforting. I do not have any doubts or concerns whilst in his company. We sit quietly looking into the water. White Feather tells me to put my hand in the water. The water feels cool and refreshing. I take my hand out, thinking I will dry it on my skirt, but there is no need: my hand is completely dry. I hear White Feather laughing. He says, 'Things are sometimes not what they seem, child, as in life appearances can be deceptive. Thus you have learned another lesson. Let us now speak of your path, Sehywha. Some days you will find it rocky, some days it will be smooth. When you sit in the quiet remember all you have seen and heard. Remember the smallest parts as well as the larger ones. Some things will be shown to you in black and white, some will be in colour. Sit with confidence, my child. Let your voice be strong and say what you see. You will know of my presence at your side and that Spirit is with you. Before you sit, prepare yourself (*smudging*). Be comfortable in what you wear. We have no objection to bare feet, as we know this is preferable to you. Make sure there is plenty of drinking water close to you. This is important: water is life! Some things, child, you have already experienced and know of, so there is no need for this one to repeat. After each experience you will feel a great tiredness descend upon you. You may even feel the need to sleep. You must rest well and drink plenty of water. This tiredness will only be for a short time, child. You will become stronger as time progresses.'

The following is a prayer that White Feather gave me to be used at the commencement of our sittings – my husband and myself have decided to commence our circle and are going to do so as soon as White Feather deems I am ready.

> *'Great Spirit, please guide us through this sitting. Allow us the strength and the knowledge for all who come here seeking the truth. Let our hearts be filled with the greatest of all, love and compassion. Lead us in our journey towards the light and love that is Spirit. Protect and guard us against anything or anyone who would wish to cause us harm.'*

A similar prayer for closure would be:

> *'We thank you, Great Spirit, for your guidance and everlasting love and for allowing us to be part of the energy channel linking with Spirit.'*

White Feather told me that there is no need to use these exact words: they are merely given as an example. He also said that it would soon be time to start our circle and that we should speak our opening and closing prayer aloud at the commencement and closure of each sitting. Sittings should be at the exact same time and place every seven days.

White Feather said: 'Our work is done for this time, child: be aware that from now on, images may appear at any time.' I must try to remember all I hear and see and write it in my notebook.

'Rest well, child.

'Yeha Noha.'

I am back... That was quite a session we had today. White Feather did all the talking: I just listened. I feel very privileged to hear his words of wisdom. He has a way with him that makes me feel very relaxed and comfortable whilst in his presence. It does not seem that we have had these sessions for less than a month: it feels more like years. When he speaks his eyes seem to glow: they are filled with trust and, although they are authoritative, their brilliance shines through. I look forward to many more lessons with him. I feel that my path ahead may not be all honey but with him guiding me I know it will certainly be interesting.

Tuesday, 27 August

It has been five days since I was asked to sit to write in

my book. Although I know White Feather is around me as I can feel his energy, he has not spoken. As soon as my mind asks why, he speaks and asks me to sit.

White Feather speaks: 'Hello, my child. It would seem that you are concerned because we do not speak. This one is always here for you, Sehywha. We do not leave your side. Have we not said before that too much learning all at once is not always best? You need time to think about all that you have been told and shown. However, now we are here we shall begin by discussing the two images you have been sent (*photographs of Mum and Dad*). Someone will come and show great interest in these images. This will be yet another step for you to take towards speaking of your experiences and the knowledge you hold in your heart. We still have far to travel, Sehywha, but the path of knowledge grows smoother. We know that you enjoy your Spiritual work, and that is as it should be. The heart, once filled with love and peace, will enable every step you take to become lighter. Do not think of things to come, child: we know of plans being made for the future commitment to Spirit. In good time the pieces will come together, and then, when the time is right, we will be there to help you. Do not forget to drink the water, Sehywha, we know your days are busy but try to remember to take the water. This is important, as it will wash away any impurities. The first day we sit and allow ourselves to be the instrument of Spirit, and allow our voice box to be used. No food should be taken from midday on that day, only water. After sitting only take a light meal. Now, child, we shall sit together and listen to the music. Fill your thoughts with happy images and feel the warmth around you like a soft blanket. Know you are loved and let contentment fill your soul. You feel light and at peace with everything and yet filled with energy. Keep these feelings as you go through your day. You have felt most of this, child, for do you not sleep better?

'Be sure to mind the images that appear before you, child. This is most important for future reference. We know that you cannot remember every single image. That is why we write to record everything we see and hear in the quiet times. These writings are your working tool and, in the fullness of time, will be of much interest to others who are treading the Spiritual path. Let your heart be light, Sehywha. Let your Spirits be uplifted so they soar high with the birds and float through the workings of your day.

'Yeha Noha.'

I thought of all White Feather had spoken of and felt elated. It is true that I have slept much more restfully since we have been communicating. I am quite excited at the thought of someone being interested in the photographs. To take a phrase from Fred Flintstone, Yabadaba-doo!

My Learning Continues

Our home circle has commenced. We sit every Wednesday evening at 7 p.m. At this stage it is purely development. We are being shown colours and images and there are quite a few 'clicks' and 'rustlings'. Nothing tangible that you could explain that would cause these noises, just a feeling of quite a lot of energy filling the room. At one of our sittings, Vic felt something or someone close to him. They seemed to come towards him and pass close to his face before disappearing into the chair beside him. He also felt something touching his arm. There are quite a few of what we call 'dinks'. These are small blobs of light that appear all around the circle area.

Each of us has had his or her own experience of images that were shown during the sitting. Our sittings usually last for about an hour, depending on what is being shown; sometimes longer. We know that we are, as previously stated, being used purely for development of our Spiritual awareness.

Thursday, 29 August

After my meditation I heard White Feather asking me to sit. As I made myself comfortable I felt the warmth of hands above my head and knew that I was being given healing. I have had some form of earache in my left ear that has been bothering me. I felt the warmth surrounding my ear, lots of tickling sensations and feelings of movement inside the ear. After the healing had finished I heard White Feather's voice saying, 'Look deep into my eyes, child (*portrait*), and breathe deeply. Feel yourself beginning to float upward. You are now at my level, Sehywha: see what I see, hear what I hear.' I felt the floor falling away and a gust of wind. I was floating over fields, rivers, roads and railway lines. Then it all became smaller as we began to soar upwards. We were so high up, I felt we were pushing against the wind. Although normally I have a fear of heights, for some reason it didn't seem to bother me. We started to descend.

'Look around you, child, remember to mind all you see and hear,' said White Feather.

We are somewhere strange, somewhere new to me but at the same time familiar. It is a strange feeling. People are walking about. Some are sitting, some are lying down. They all have sad, unsmiling faces. There is a feeling of nothingness everywhere. Everyone looks lethargic and shuffles about with no energy. White Feather says, 'We cannot stay here long, Sehywha. You will lose too much energy and tire quickly. There is a purpose in our visit. Perhaps you have already seen someone you recognise.' I can hear crying, and someone is shouting 'Where am I?' A feeling of utter sadness is all around. There are so many people. I am aware of a feeling of heaviness, almost of not being able to breathe. Then we are leaving. White Feather tells me to close my eyes. Before I do, I see the image of the soldier in the red tunic and white helmet I saw in my kitchen. He says, 'Help me, please, help me!' We are floating upward again, moving faster and faster. I begin to lose the feeling of not being able to breathe. I am so pleased we were leaving: this place is awful, indescribable.

'You know of this place, do you not, child? This is where the work for Spirit begins. In the beginning we start with one: two if you feel ready. Spirit knows you are willing, child, but we must also take care of the physical body. Healing will always be given after each connection. You will feel a sort of heaviness in both yourself and in the air around you when you begin. Thus you will know that the work commences. Rest now, Sehywha. The next time we speak we will make the arrangements necessary for the work to begin.

'Yeha Noha.'

My journey today was to those who, in White Feather's words, 'tread the dark path'. These are lost souls, those who have passed over but for one reason or another refuse to recognise the fact of their mortal death. These poor souls need to be made aware of what has happened to them and where they are in order to progress onward into Spirit. It is hard for some souls when they pass over to accept that they have left their mortal body behind and are now a free Spirit. Since we have started our 'rescue' missions, the most prominent thing that crops up time after time is lack of knowledge whilst on earth as to what happens after death. Those with whom we have spoken, when they appear at our rescue sessions, are confused: it takes quite a lot of explanation to help them understand where they are. Some accept more easily than others. Some can get quite stroppy and others, when they realise that there is no returning to their 'life' as it was, are absolutely devastated. We always try to glean as much information from them as possible. This is for our own records. We usually have a tape recorder running so that we can listen to it afterwards to ensure we had done all that we could have for that person. We know we have been successful in our explanation to them at the end of their visit because they always see someone they know coming towards them, or a white light that beckons them. We ask them their name and where they lived, what year it is to them and the last thing that they remember. From the few facts we are given we try to 'jog their memory' as it were, so that we can then work our way forward to their Spirit's departure date. Some remember being in hospital, feeling really poorly, whilst others have been in a fire or some kind of accident. Some are within the last twenty years or so and some go back further. One chap, who had been a postman over seventy years ago, kept saying that his wife would be worried about him and that his dinner would be waiting for him. He appeared to have had a heart attack whilst delivering the post and just died whilst doing his round.

I do not think that we have had any failures. One lady left us suddenly in the midst of being told what had happened to her, but we were told later in one of my sittings to write with White Feather that she had arrived in Spirit and that all was well.

I hope that this explanation is sufficient for you to understand what we call a 'rescue'.

Monday, 2 September

Today there is a great energy about in the lounge. Several times I have been aware of someone just standing, looking at me. I see them out of the corner of my eye. I do not turn and look because I know that if I did they would disappear. I can hear voices too, lots of chattering and laughing. (Seems like the makings of a party.) White Feather's image smiles down on me and I feel quite relaxed and at peace. I hear White Feather asking me please to sit. After I have been seated for a while White Feather speaks to me: 'Remember our journeys, Sehywha. One in particular we wish to speak of now. Remember the crossroads? The different coloured paths; do you remember the colour you chose? Your choice was the blue path and you were told that we would take this path to see where it led, on another visit. It is this path that we will now take. Close your eyes, child, listen to the music, feel the drum as it beats softly, beating in time with our breathing.'

I can feel myself beginning to float upward and then forward. I can feel the wind as it rushes past. We are now descending. We are in the clearing in the woods at the crossroads. Of all the different coloured paths the blue one shines the brightest.

White Feather: 'Now, Sehywha, our journey begins.' We start to walk along the blue path. When we have walked a little way White Feather stops me by holding up his hand. 'Be sure to mind all you hear and see, child: this will be for future reference and should be recorded as it is seen.' We move on. At the end of the path is a large building, similar to the first one (the hall of arrivals). It has many steps. We enter. I can hear music being played very softly. There is a gentle breeze that moves what look like muslin drapes in a soft, swaying motion. These are a very pale blue and draped in huge swirls. There are faces here of every race. They seem to be working in cubicles made of the muslin swirls. We stop at one of the cubicles. There is a man standing there, about my height and quite sturdily built. His hair is thinning and he has rosy cheeks and bright blue eyes behind gold-rimmed specs (another surprise – didn't think they wore glasses in Spirit!). He has a small pointed beard and a lovely beaming smile.

'This is your healing guide, Sehywha. He is an excellent doctor and will be with you when you have your healing sessions. You will call him Dominic.' The doctor, Dominic, led me to a chair and I sat down. He sat opposite me and took both my hands in his. I felt the heat of his hands immediately: they felt like they were on fire. I could not look at my hands to see just what was happening because I could not take my eyes away from those of the doctor. I felt a great surge of energy go up my arms into my body. The heat was getting so intense that I could not bear it. Just when I was about to ask him to stop he gently turned my hands, palms upwards, and closed my fingers over to form a fist. Finally my hands were placed in my lap. The doctor went behind me and I felt the heat of his hands right down to my feet. I heard a voice telling me that I was now ready and that when the healing work commenced, my new-found friend Dominic would be beside me. Before we left I thanked Dominic for all his love and help and for his assistance in the future.

White Feather: 'Have you any thoughts, child? We see questions that need an answer.' I asked when the healing could commence and also about the rescue work. I still needed to know more about White Feather himself, his life on earth and how he lived it; could he tell me more?

White Feather: 'The answer to the first question: healing will commence as soon as the first person arrives at your door in need of it. The rescue work goes well and will continue after you return from the log cabin. (*We are going on holiday to Cornwall on 14 September.*) For the answer to your third question concerning this one, you must look in the hall of books. (*Library?*) There you will find some of the answers you seek. We know that you have an appetite for learning and it is here you will read about me and my people. There you will find some of the answers you seek. More answers will follow in the fullness of time. This will be another path for you to follow in the old ways. Our purpose, in the small amounts of time we spend together communicating, is for you to learn about yourself, child, and your path on Mother Earth. Time is given to you, Sehywha, not to me.'

I am now back in the lounge. The last question I had for White Feather concerned the name for our new home. (*We are hoping to move to Cornwall at some stage in the future.*) White Feather: 'The choice of name for your lodge is yours, Sehywha: call it what you will. Perhaps you need to go back to our first communication to find the answer. Now you must rest, child; do not forget to drink the water.'

After today's lesson, whilst writing in my daily log, I heard his voice and very faintly the word 'Sarawak'.

My visits to the 'other side' today were indescribable: I know I have written everything down as it happened but I feel I have not done it justice. It is everything I thought of as Heaven and yet it is not. It is one hundred times more beautiful and totally unbelievable. Again, who would possibly believe what has just happened to me? I must not doubt what I have seen: for one I would not be in White Feather's good books, and for another how could I possibly put it down to an 'it's all in the mind' type of thing? When I look out of my lounge window there are no colours that could match what I have seen on my travels with White Feather. The grass here is dull; the grass on the other side is a beautiful emerald green and has what I can only describe as lustre. As for my meeting with Dominic, well, words fail me: all I can say is, *Wow!*

The question concerning a name for our new home came about when my husband asked me to speak to White Feather with regard to calling it 'White Feather Lodge'. It would appear that he did not like this idea and so suggested Sarawak. At the time of my writing this book, my husband has his diploma for hypnotherapy and his client list is growing. He has named his practice 'Sarawak Hypnotherapy', after the name given him by White Feather.

Tuesday, 3 September

We began today with thoughts and prayers for all those in need of healing (we have a healing book in which we enter the names of people who we have been told need healing: this is what we call absent healing). White Feather told me that there would be two people coming who would be eager to join our circle. There is much energy in our lodge (this is White Feather's name for our home) and he said that this energy would grow even more.

White Feather: 'You are more than ready now, child, and capable of many things. You will find that your intuition grows in strength. Many daily tasks will be done easily and tirelessly. Thoughts will come to you at any time concerning your Spirit work. We know it will not always be the right time but with your ability you will be able to store these in your "deal with later" box. Your mind now, child, has the benefit of knowing that this one will be close to you always and, if a situation or problem arises that seems beyond your comprehension, this one will assist you in finding the answer. In all things, child, fill your heart and thoughts with love. Before you begin your healing moments be sure to prepare yourself mentally. The thoughts of love and the desire to help those in need will bring your healing guide, Dominic. His great passion for healing the sick and your ability to be guided by him will benefit both the one who receives the healing and yourself. As always, child, drink the water and know that we are here for you.

'Yeha Noha.'

It seems that Spirit may wish to use me in some sort of healing capacity. I shall put it to the back of my mind for now until they let me know what it is exactly they want me for.

I know that my awareness is growing in leaps and bounds. I immediately know when White Feather is around me. At one time if I had a question, I would ask that question and perhaps some time later he would answer me. It seems that lately when I ask a question he is there with the answer straight away. This, he tells me, is due to my increasing awareness of Spirit and my eagerness to learn more. I seem to get quite a lot of answers to problems and questions whilst I'm in the shower. My husband also seems to get answers to certain problems when he is in the shower. We laughed a lot about this and jokingly said, If you have a problem, take a shower. Whilst White Feather and I were having one of my lessons a few days later, he suddenly said to me, whilst talking about something else, 'Water is a conductor, you know. When you are taking a bath or under running water you are more relaxed and therefore feel Spirit's presence even more.' Something else I did not know!

The next sitting with White Feather concerns suggestions to help my husband develop further. He has to overcome a few little hurdles. One of his problems is just plain old relaxation. Clearing his mind of everything and just sitting quietly is quite an effort for him. The actual sitting still is not a problem: what he finds difficult is clearing his mind. All sorts of things go through his mind whilst sitting and, as much as he tries, he cannot manage to just make his mind go blank. The following will explain. My husband's guide is Abraham and is of African/French descent. He calls my husband '*Mon Ami*', which means my friend.

Wednesday, 4 September

I got up just after my husband left for work, around 6.45 a.m., and started my meditation. I felt White Feather's presence and that he wished to speak with me.

'No teachings this time, Sehywha, only observations on how best to help our friend (*my husband*) to overcome his inability to concentrate on Spiritual matters. No doubt my old friend Abraham will help him but you must help him too, child. Now is the time to show him how to sit in the quiet with peaceful thoughts. Listen to the music together (*we have a tape called* Crystal Healing *that we use for circle time, played very softly, just in the background, as it were*). Set aside a time to do this together. My understanding knows that our friend has to work long hours and that he is tired. If he sleeps when you sit it is no matter. He will receive healing in this time and be shown images of the peace and restfulness you already know. He has put the teachings of your earlier sittings with those now in Spirit (*Ruth and Leslie Bone*) at the back of his consciousness. He has the ability to communicate with the Spirit and this he will develop, but first he must learn to still the restlessness inside and be patient. A tree does not grow overnight. We must guide him along his path, child, until such time as he can hear the voice and words of Abraham. This Spirit is a great teacher and has many words of wisdom to give our friend, once he learns to listen. As you already know, child, this one is here to guide you but, because it is imperative that you continue on your path to use your knowledge and the gifts you have been given, we have taken counsel and agreed that, until such time as our friend can hear and speak with Abraham, this one will assist through you. We know our friend reads your writings, Sehywha: to this end explanations will come from these, from this one to him by way of the writings. When you sit in the quiet together, ask him to fill his thoughts with a peaceful image, to hold onto this and to try not to be distracted from what he sees. Tell him to let every other thought that tries to break up this image fade away without thinking of it too deeply. Remind him that the sooner he learns to accept the quiet, the quicker will come all the knowledge he will need to tread his path. Our friend knows which path he needs to follow but to do this, child, he must learn to be "in charge" of his thoughts and to disregard any other that may try to enter. He can do this, for he is strong. He must tell himself this at all times. To do his Spirit work and achieve his goal from the task he has set himself, he must be clear of mind.

Once he can do this, the teachings he will be given

will become easier to absorb. So, my child, the words are written. Ask our friend to read and reread what we have spoken of; to free his mind of the happenings of the day; to put any anxieties he has to one side and to think only of the Spiritual work he wishes to follow. Just as a dry cloth, when put into water, will absorb as much as it is able, so the quiet mind absorbs teaching. His future on the Spiritual path begins with patience. Once the ground is prepared the sowing will commence. Your help in all this, child, will be given as always without question. The great Spirit smiles on you, Sehywha. Abraham is nodding his head and smiling also. You are greatly loved, child, and much needed for your Spiritual work. To this end we know you are willing. Rest, child, and remember the water.

'Yeha Noha.'

From this sitting it would appear that I will supply the energy when my husband and I sit together in meditation. This will enable him to progress further along the Spiritual path. My husband finds it very hard to clear his mind whilst meditating and, I know he will not mind my saying (because he knows it is true), that he does lack patience. He wants it all to happen there and then. He longs for the day he will be able to hear Abraham's voice. I am sure he will in time: he is already seeing little sparks of light around the home and has heard his name called, but because it was gone in a flash he thought he imagined it. Since this happened we have received verification that it was not his imagination. This was very exciting news indeed, and, moreover, knowing that his work for Spirit had truly begun gave my husband the extra bit of confidence he needed.

Thursday, 5 September

Sitting later today. (Had trouble changing the bed linen – the duvet misbehaved itself!) Heard White Feather asking me to sit with my book. White Feather: 'We shall not keep you this time, child, as we know it is a busy day for you. We have talked of many things and seen many places together and now the picture is whole. It may take a little time, Sehywha, before our friend is ready to begin the work. To this end it is being asked that you continue your meditation together. Abraham and this one will be there with you, child.'

It was suggested that our next meditation be on the following Sunday, as soon as we arose and before eating – a glass of water only to be taken. I was also told to shield the room from sunlight and from all happenings outside the home. From this sitting Spirit would be able to judge our reactions to what was being given.

Sunday, 9 September

White Feather has just spoken about the sitting we did at 8.15 a.m. this morning. I was used to boost the energy so that Vic could relax and be comfortable with images he was being given. Confirmation was given on the colours shown to him and that Abraham had managed to 'open the door a crack' to future communications between himself and Vic. Confirmation for Vic was the name 'George' given to him during the meditation. This was an uncle of my husband, now in Spirit. We both felt very elated with this message from White Feather and it gave Vic that little bit of reassurance he needed.

Monday, 10 September

We started today with prayers for healing and for world peace, something that very much concerns our Spiritual friends.

White Feather: 'All goes well, child. We still have much work to do with out friend (*Vic*). Abraham thanks you for your energy and support for our friend. Our findings are: he (*Vic*) has the ability to communicate with Spirit, which we already knew. He has much emotion built up inside him, which he needs to let go. He has conflicting thoughts. This is another barrier we must overcome. If we can clear the emotion the thoughts will settle. He has shown that he can, when the situation requires, be still. Until such time as he can hear Abraham's voice, you, Sehywha, will be our connection. Sit in the quiet together: use your energies to help him overcome his anxieties. His future work (*hypnotherapy*) helping people to overcome their problems depends upon this. He must have the quiet mind to do this work. He knows that the message given in the sitting was true, as were the images. In order to help others he must first help himself. He must believe in himself, child. He questions what he sees (*colours, images*) and in so doing he is erecting barriers. He sometimes asks, "Is it my imagination or is it being given by Spirit?" Again we say he must believe in himself and his capabilities. We shall speak again soon, child.

'Yeha Noha.'

We have now reached the stage where we are ready to start our home circle. White Feather has asked that it be set at the same time and day each week. The first sitting will be of enlightenment. We hope to invite others to join us soon but for now Vic and I will sit every Wednesday evening at 7 p.m. White Feather, realising that we have concerns over who to ask to join us in our circle, gave the following: 'We realise that you have concerns regarding the choice of who should or should not sit with you, child. Do not let these concerns cloud your consciousness. Take your time: we will guide you. We understand also that you have concerns about the speed of happenings around you, that you wish for all matters concerning Spirit to be true and positive, as we do, and as they shall be. You know your path, child, for you have been shown the work that is before you both in the mortal and immortal. Your writings of our time spent together grow, child. We still have many matters to discuss, many things yet to see. Life is for learning, child, do not forget this. Your writings will be of great comfort to you and will help you grow in knowledge of Spirit, thereby giving you some of the answers needed when you speak to others. These writings are a record of our time spent together, Sehywha, and as such should be regarded as a working tool for you.'

I spent the rest of the day thinking about what White Feather had said, trying to understand fully the meaning of his words. I understood what he meant about asking others to join our home circle. It was the last part that I had difficulty with: the bit about speaking to others concerning Spirit. I could no more get to my feet and speak and answer questions about Spirit than I could fly. Don't get me wrong, I love to hear about Spirit and to listen to others talking about their experiences, but I could never do that myself. I seem to have something inside me that freezes if I feel that I am in the spotlight.

Then it suddenly dawned on me what I could do – or perhaps Spirit gave me the idea. I would put all that I had learned from White Feather into book form. That way I could say exactly how I felt about what had happened to me without the embarrassment of actually speaking. Having made up my mind, I had no idea that the amount of writing that I would be doing would amount to (to date four A5 ruled books – amounting to some 300-odd pages) such a task. But the more I thought about it the more the idea grew. At this time I did not know that my guide had a few more ideas up his sleeve concerning plans for my future enlightenment...

Because of the 'closeness' I felt with White Feather I was determined to find out a little more about his life on earth. This is where I enlisted the help of someone I felt could help me with this. In a magazine that advertises anything to do with the mind, body and Spirit that takes place in the West Country, I found a gentleman by the name of Kerys Laughing Bear. He was a Celtic Amerindian Crow who was a teacher, reader and healer in Native American Spiritualism, as taught to him by his father. Kerys did his first vision quest when he was thirteen and has been walking the path and working with the powers and animals since before then and it is a part of his life. Kerys ran various workshops in Devon, amongst which was 'Shamanic Pathways'. I decided to write to Kerys to see if he could help me with my quest to find out more about my guide.

I duly sent my letter to Kerys and a few days later he telephoned me. He said he would be writing to me with what he had found out about White Feather but needed to know a little about how I knew my guide. I brought Kerys up to speed on all I knew about White Feather and then said goodbye and told him I looked forward to hearing from him.

A couple of weeks later I received my first letter from Kerys. I say first because we have corresponded since that time. At the time of writing Kerys is in New Zealand and has been since last October. I have had one phone call and a letter from him and I know he will be in contact again. I consider Kerys to be a very good friend. He understands why I am here and where my future lies, and I have no doubt that Kerys has much he could teach me. Kerys, to me, is also a brother because – perhaps it will be hard for others to understand – we have kindred feelings, as I am about to tell you now.

Kerys wrote the following:

Dear Geraldine,

Apologies for the delay, life has been hectic, however I am pleased and happy to gift you with the learning I've been granted by White Feather.

It seems that you are in a 'granddaughter' situation/position that is also a 'favoured one' situation. It seems that the connection is also because 'medicine' sometimes jumps a generation or two and the strength of the teacher/tutor is also dependant on the ability of the receiver. Obviously your intercommunications are on a 'clear line' with each other. I didn't actually ask about direct in-time contact between the two of you in the past, but it would not surprise me if it existed.

Anyway, here is what we have been communicating about as regards White Feather:

He was born in 1823 up along the Wind River in Autumn Camp (Wyoming, south of Yellowstone). During his childhood his tribe travelled, camped and hunted down as far as North Colorado (Fort Collins area), west to about Salt Lake, north as far as Southern Montana (south of the Yellowstone river) and east to the Black hills, the Badlands and Western Nebraska.

During this time he went thro' the normal rites of passage and initiation. He also married, had children and at least one grandchild that he saw.

During his life he was not a mystic but a warrior/healer. As a healer he was what they call today in the tribe an 'Indian doctor' rather than a shamanic healer. This is an important definition. He did ride in war and raiding parties and did kill, but he also 'counted coup', which counts higher. In 1864 during a confrontation with the whites (it is not clear whether this was encroaching settlers or the US Army, since the Civil War was also on at that time) he took a wound in the right-hand side, which became infected; he subsequently died of this infection, although he did make it back to his village. He has been around a few times also and part of his work is to 'open doorways'; hence his work with you.

His personal power animal (totem) is the elk and his clan was the dog.

He also had another name and it may be that he will give this to you at a later stage.

'Yeha Noha' is a goodbye, 'fare thee well' sort of thing, but I do not speak Shoshone! 'Sehywha' is like 'little one', 'my child' etc.: an affectionate dimi-name.

As far as you are concerned you are here to be a gatherer, a weaver of threads, a sharer, a tale-teller, a speaker of the word, a carrier of ideas.

Also you have work to do on travelling between the worlds (this is not dream work or projection), working your way through the 'doorways' and being (sometimes) very surprised but learning by the experimental journey. (N.B. These worlds are real: you eat, breathe and can, if you get hurt, bleed. Although part of the shamanic work, you can still walk them even if you are not a shaman.)

Also, Geraldine, you are here to learn about life and to understand death. You will need to explore and learn with the power animals/totems. In this respect you will need to learn to communicate with them, travel with them and see through them and eventually 'put on their skin', although you will be unlikely to be a 'skin walker'. For this you may well have to find someone to train and teach you.

Remember also that this world you are in now is real, too: sometimes people get lost in the other worlds!

Anyway, Geraldine, walk your path bravely, stand tall, laugh and enjoy.

Mitakoye Oyasin *(all our relations)*

Kerys Laughing Bear.

P.S. Please feel free to contact me for anything else.

P.P.S. Work with black, red, yellow and white.

I was absolutely amazed by the letter I received from Kerys. The first thing that hit me was the date of 1864. This was the date that White Feather had given me in one of our early sittings. He was forty-one when he died: this was something else that astounded me because his image (portrait) seemed to show an older man. However, I soon realised that the image showed him as I see him now, not as he was when he passed over. After all, it has been 141 years since his passing.

I also felt very excited by what Kerys had told me, about the work that was ahead of me. A month or so later my husband and I visited a psychic fair in Marlborough and it was here that I met Merlynne White Bear and found out about a shamanic healing course that she ran. I felt that I had been 'led' to this gathering for this exact purpose, to learn about shamanic work, and knew instinctively that this was where I would meet my power animals and learn the 'old ways'.

But that is another story: I will tell you all about this later. For now I wish to get back to my daily lessons with

White Feather, about our many talks and journeys together.

Thursday, 12 September

We are off on holiday to Cornwall this coming Saturday so at this sitting I asked White Feather about our daily talks whilst I am away. The answer was, 'We have a true understanding between us, child. There is no need for words. The message comes from the heart. It matters not that you leave my image in your lodge whilst you are away (*I had told White Feather that I could not take his picture with me in case it got broken in transit*); you feel my energy all around you. You also see my image at the times we communicate. It is good that you take the writings with you (*my book*). These will sustain you in the knowledge of all we have spoken of. You may speak to me at any time you wish. Sehywha, we shall not call upon you whilst you are resting unless you need answers to questions. Look upon the next ten days as a rest time. Fill your being with the fresh sea air and let the soft winds blow away any cares you may have. You already know, child, that the place you go to is very close to Spirit. Feel the earth, the rocks and the trees. Feel the vibrancy entering your very soul. We shall have one more sitting before you leave, child. It will be a memory to hold in your heart and to think on for all our future work together.

'Yeha Noha.'

The memory that White Feather spoke of on our last sitting was of my father. He appeared in my lounge looking very well. I touched him, gave him a hug and was immediately drawn to tears. He felt completely solid. What I touched was solid, not a mirage or ghostly in any way. He was shown to me in his earthly body and not as energy or Spirit. I have not forgotten this and I never will. It was the best gift ever.

On the last day of our holiday we called in to see my husband's cousin, Martin, and his wife Sue. Martin is an animal healer/horse whisperer and a developing medium. Sue is a past life researcher. We had loads to talk about, as it was quite a few years since Vic and Martin had last met. All I can say of our meeting is, '*Wow!*' The amount of energy around the dinner table was so much so that we had to stop talking about Spiritual matters. It was absolutely incredible: both Martin and myself felt the energy between us. The hairs on his arms stood up. I had goose bumps and, at one stage, when Martin stood he nearly fell over: such was the vibration. I had never met Martin and Sue before that day, although I had met Martin's dad, David.

Martin gave me a lot of information concerning things that had happened in my past: that I had lost a child through miscarriage when I was twenty-one; that I had a surgical scar running down my left side (I had a hernia operation when I was seventeen) and much, much more. It was a truly wonderful day and one we promised to repeat in the near future.

There is a book written by Jane E White called *Spiritual Guides in the West Country* that has an article about Martin and Sue in it. There are also writings about Steve (Martin's twin brother) and his wife Gwyn, who live in Weston Super Mare, incorporated into this book. Steve is a psychic artist and medium, whilst Gwyn does painting, printmaking and is also a very Spiritual lady. I will tell you more about Steve and Gwyn later in the book.

Whilst we were on holiday in Cornwall we went one evening to Bude Spiritual Church. After the service, a visiting medium by the name of Colin Marshall gave a few messages to my husband. These took the form of seeing a man in uniform surrounded by water and the name George. This was my husband's Uncle George, now in Spirit, who had been in the navy. There was also an old school friend and the image of a shiny new spade. The latter my husband took to represent his hypnotherapy course, which he had started, and the Spirit saying 'get on with it'. All in all, when we got home at the end of our holiday we felt that it had been a worthwhile trip.

Lessons and Journeys

Monday 23, September

After meditation White Feather came through straight away.

'My dear child, we trust you feel both physically and Spiritually refreshed after your visit to the place known for its strength of Spirit. Does not your heart feel uplifted? Your energy grows daily, Sehywha, this you already know. You feel great expectations of excitement that you cannot explain to anyone. Only those such as yourself who have the gift know this feeling. There is much ahead for you, child: we know this feeling also. The strength of your energy and your vibration will be felt by many. Those who understand the way of Spirit will recognise you without being spoken to. Of course, my child, there will also be those who do not see the signs and thus will give you the name of "that strange woman". Do not let this deter you. Sehywha. You are aware of those who do not believe in Spirit. The one you call "Martin"' felt your energy and if you follow the path that is being made for your earthly future (*move to the West Country*) you will be nearer to this man. There is great power between you. Think of all the energy and vibrations that will be in one place at one time. Spirit is indeed wonderful, my child; we too feel uplifted with these thoughts. Very soon comes another who also has the energy. We know that when he comes your lodge will fill to the roof with this energy.

'Do not be afraid of the physical feelings you have at the present, child (*this is in reference to the tingling in hands and the goose bumps all over my arms, shoulders and neck*); these are all part of the energy that is with you. Strange names, places and events will enter your thoughts. Speak them, child; all will become clear when the answers are given. We feel great joy with the progress you are making, Sehywha: these gifts are precious and must be treated as such. We have many matters to speak of, child, but for now we wait. Too much too soon can be confusing. We will take our time so that you understand. If this one's words of explanation are not understood you must speak. Enough for now, child; rest, drink the water and enjoy your surprise.' (*Do not know what this means.*)

'Yeha Noha.'

Two pieces of information given to me later in the day, concerning Martin and Sue, prompted me to write to them to give them what I had received. At some stage, Martin would be offered an assignment in Canada (horses): a combined holiday/work thing (fare to be paid by person seeking his help). Sue (who is currently studying past lives, reincarnation and psychometric readings) was going to increase her awareness threefold.

Tuesday, 24 September

Before writing about the next sitting with White Feather, the events of Tuesday, 24 September should be explained. This was the surprise White Feather had spoken of.

We had a visit from Martin's brother, Steve, who is a psychic artist, and his wife Gwyn. They arrived around five. We had supper and then began discussing Spirit. Steve had brought a few drawings with him. Two were for Vic and were recognised as two aunts who had passed to Spirit a while back. The one for me was of a North American Indian (which Steve had drawn on 22 September). It appeared to be my guide, White Feather, and although Steve had portrayed him a little differently to the way Lynn had, the likeness was there. In Steve's drawing White Feather was wearing a war bonnet, whereas in the one that Lynn had done his only adornment was the four white feathers he wore in his hair. Nevertheless, it was a striking picture.

We had such a wonderful evening: there were coloured specks of light dancing around the room and the energy vibrations were just fantastic. Steve and Gwyn were given a small reading from White Feather (through me). Again, Canada was mentioned. It was discovered later that Steve and Gwyn had been told before in a reading that they would be going to Canada at some stage, to continue their Spiritual work. The figure five was quoted. Five people would be going to Canada.

The evening ended on a high. Everyone felt so elated they did not want it to end, but because Steve and Gwyn had quite a journey ahead we had to bring it to a close. I can tell you that when I finally got to bed a little after midnight, I had trouble getting to sleep. As I was starting to doze off I heard White Feather's voice: 'Sleep well, child,' and then he laughed and was gone.

Wednesday, 25 September

After last evening's experiences I slept in until 8.30 a.m.

When I got up I showered and washed my hair, still feeling a little drained and lethargic. However, after an hour or so I started to feel a little better. Told myself I would have a lazy day today after meditation. I would listen to my music and do my crocheting (one of my hobbies: I crochet squares which I sew together to make bed quilts). However, as always, plans did not materialise. At 11 a.m. I was asked to sit.
White Feather: 'Now you are feeling refreshed, my child, we wish to speak about our visit to your lodge. First our apologies to the one called Steve, for leaving his question unanswered. Time prevented this, we wished not to stay with you too long. He will understand the reasoning here. For you, my child, the explanation is simple. It has been a long time since we used your physical body and voice box. We know you have given permission for this to happen but to have stayed longer would have taken too much of your energy and may have caused discomfort to you. Rest assured, child, there will be other times when the need arises to call on you.

'Now, my child, a message for the one whose question was not answered. When we have spoken we wish you to give him this. Write exactly what you hear.' (*Now have to get separate sheets of paper for Steve. Wrote four pages, will post off to Steve tomorrow.*)

Message for Steve: 'My son, we beg your forgiveness for seeming to ignore your question on your future work. Our time spent with Sehywha was sparing because it has been a long time since we used her for this specific work. We know you understand the ways of Spirit, thus no further explanation is necessary. Sehywha has been in my charge since her birth; she is as a daughter to me. You felt this when you drew my image. We will let no harm come to this child; indeed she is well protected because of the work she has to do. Now, my son, the answer to your question. Your future lies in the images that you produce. We are sure that your Guides have told you this. You also have the ability to see all around you. We know that time is important to you: you need time for your daily work as well as time for your Spiritual work. We also know that you need payment for what you do. Your daytime work leaves very little hours for your Spiritual work. No matter. Most work given for Spirit is given freely but there are certain circumstances in which you can ask for and receive payment. You, my son, have given freely of your time to Spirit for a very long time. Now Spirit wishes to repay, to help you further along the Path of Light. To this we would say to you: We have seen the encouragement you give to the fair lady (*Gwyn*). She too is very aware, and with your help will progress further. Your future is combined with hers. Give more readings, together, to those who ask. Do not concern yourself, my son, for your future is very, very bright. Leave the healing to the tall one (*Martin*). For now concentrate on your images. The advice you gave to Sehywha concerning her writings can also apply to you. Put your images and thoughts on paper (*book*). People of the Earth seek answers to many, many questions concerning Spirit. You, my son, will help answer some of these questions through your experiences.

'Yeha Noha.'

White Feather continued after I had written the message to Steve: 'Abraham is very pleased with the progress our friend makes (*Vic*). There will be more shown to him as time passes and his energy level rises. Now, my child, you must rest. You must eat to replenish your physical needs; we shall look after the Spiritual side. Rest well, Sehywha. We shall speak again soon.

'Yeha Noha.'

A little explanation regarding Steve's reading: Steve is a charge nurse of a local hospice/nursing home in Weston. He gets a little frustrated at times because he cannot give as much time to his Spiritual work as he would like. Steve needed to know if he should carry on with his drawings or perhaps change his path. Steve rang me a couple of days later after he had received the reading from White Feather and told me that he understood absolutely what White Feather meant. He has decided to write a book about his psychic work as and when he gets the time. He will stay with his drawings. At the time of writing this book, Steve has progressed in leaps and bounds. He has teamed up with a fellow psychic, Ben Gater, and does demonstrations around the south. Ben does the readings of people in the audience whilst Steve draws what he is being given from Spirit. Sometimes it is a relative who has passed to Spirit; other times it could be a guide for the person Ben is reading. Steve still has trouble finding enough time to do all he wants to do. He is still nursing during the day: that will always have to come first. He is also trying to fit his Spiritual work and book writing in what is left of his time. Steve says things get a little hectic at times but, somehow or other, he manages to fit everything in. Gwyn, too, is receiving more demands for her paintings.

Thursday, 26 September

I have been up since 7 a.m. expecting a visit from White Feather. It is now 9.30 a.m.: still no sign. I am very fidgety, cannot sit still. I have a sense of expectation. Something is going to happen: the room is full of energy. Heard some loud clicks and saw sparks of different colours everywhere. I have felt things before but not like this, I now have goose bumps and the back of my neck has gone quite cold. Still no sign of White Feather. I am going to have my breakfast and then study the Runes. Steve has suggested I learn to read the Runes as an additional string to my bow.

Thursday evening

Abraham spoke for the first time, through me. Vic taped the message from him. This message was to do with my husband's Spiritual development.

I now know why there was so much going on today: they were preparing for Abraham's visit.

Monday, 30 September

Sat today at 9.45 a.m. Heard White Feather's voice: 'Come, child, we will sit by the lake and discuss present and future developments. In the quiet time we can reflect on the happenings whilst we fill our hearts with the perfect peace and beauty around us.' Once again I hear the soft music of the pipes and then the beat of the drum. I begin to float and feel myself rising higher and higher. I do not open my eyes until my feet touch the ground.

White Feather is already there. He is with a gentleman I instantly recognise from his portrait: it is Abraham. As I approach he turns and smiles at me and thanks me for allowing him to use my vibration to meet his friend, Mon Ami (Vic). He tells me that there is much more he needs to say and asks permission to speak through me again. I tell him he is most welcome to come as often as he needs.

He thanks me and says: 'My name for you will be Lady; this will enable Mon Ami to recognise the messenger.' Abraham stands up to leave and I am surprised at his size. He is quite a small man, not at all as I imagined him to be. The only knowledge I have of him is that he was of African/French descent, and that he was a teacher in his earthly life; it would seem that his teaching continues. He smiles at me, bows, turns to White Feather and bows to him before walking away. White Feather: 'You are thinking how different Abraham is to the image you had in your thoughts, child. He tells me to say to you, "Small is beautiful." '

We sit quietly by the lake, feeling the peacefulness of this lovely place. It is relaxing but at the same time fills me with exuberance.

White Feather: 'All goes well, child. Sometimes matters do not move quickly enough for our friend (*Vic*); he must be patient, for all will bear fruit in good time. There is a great difference in time between our worlds. We already know of things to come and thus say to you, Do not concern yourself. Greet each new dawn with renewed vigour for the day ahead, love in your heart for all and a prayer on your tongue for all that you give and are given.

'We know of your concerns and sometimes frustrated thoughts of your sister, child. She is being helped but takes too many matters upon herself. Until she learns to sit in the quiet and open herself up to the help she is given, very little of that help will be received. She asks why she cannot feel Spirit. The answer is that Spirit is ready and most willing to help but cannot until the barrier is lifted.

'We are now considering time to be spent in work for the souls who walk the dark path (*rescue work*). We know of all things and wish not to take too much away from our friend's learning time (*Vic*). The learning time is important for the future, so we ask that when the time is right, we use a specific time for this work. This you will know in advance of our sitting (*day, evening, time etc.*). This will enable our friend (*Vic*) to plan his learning schedule (*Vic is well into his hypnotherapy studies*). Rest now, child. As always, we are with you. Do not forget to drink the water.

'Yeha Noha.'

A word of explanation. The first explanation: my sister. Unfortunately my sister is always suffering from one thing or another. She has one ongoing problem: insomnia. She has about four hours' sleep per night. I think it is because she is a worrier. She worries about her children, her grandchildren and if her friends have problems, they are her problems too. I found a Spiritualist church in her area and told her to go for a healing. She did go, once, but when I asked if she had been back she said that it was too much of a journey on the bus, and that anyway she did not relish going out on dark evenings.

The second explanation concerns the rescue work that White Feather spoke about. Souls who walk the dark path are those who have crossed over and left their physical bodies behind, but as yet do not realise what has happened to them. Their last memory, before they passed, is the very last thing they were doing: either lying in bed ill, or in the case of accidents, driving along a road, or being in a building that was on fire. Some have the memory of being in water, in an aeroplane or even mountain climbing. Every passing is different. Some know what is happening to them and accept the fact. Some even look forward to passing because it means an end to perhaps months of pain and suffering: the thought of 'going home', as it were, fills them with calm and peace.

There are others who do not understand what has happened to them. They know that they are not where they used to be and are confused and frightened. These are the ones who need our help in order to recognise that they have left their physical bodies behind and are now free Spirits. This is where the rescue work begins. These poor lost souls (and indeed many others) are brought to our circle to be helped to realise what has actually happened to them. Once they accept that what they are being told is the truth, they usually shed a few tears, not so much for themselves as for those they have left behind. Once they have calmed themselves they either see a bright light beckoning them, or a friend or relative who has already passed to Spirit comes to escort them safely over to their new life. Sometimes some of these lost souls are very hard to convince, not ever having had any belief in the afterlife whilst on earth, but it is worth every minute we spend with them to know at the end of our talk to them that they are no longer lost souls and have gone to join the other free Spirits. How long each one takes to accept what is being said governs the time limit and the energy of the medium. If they are what we call 'easy' rescues we have two or three at circle time. If they are difficult then there is usually just one.

Having said all of this, the next sitting with White Feather will be self-explanatory.

Tuesday, 1 October

White Feather came later today, thought he was not coming so I started the ironing. Hearing his voice I switched the iron off, made myself comfortable in my chair and waited.

White Feather: 'We wish to speak of sitting in circle, child. We hear your words concerning the right time for you and our friend (*Vic*). We ask that the time be set for the third day (*Wednesday*) at sunset (*about 7 p.m.*). Please remove all noise that may cause disturbance (*phone, doorbell etc.*). You should use the blue light for this purpose, Sehywha. (*We have a blue shaded table lamp, in which we have placed a blue bulb.*) We wish to bring two lost souls who tread the dark path (*rescue*); when the last one has gone we shall come to take away any darkness that remains around you and your lodge. You may drink before sitting but no food. We know that we have come before when you have already eaten but this is different and may cause sickness to the stomach. After the sitting you may eat lightly; indeed you will enjoy it and feel much refreshed. Our friend (*Vic*) may also drink but no food. He has to be aware and alert. He may feel the need to exercise his breathing for a short time before we begin. The souls have been chosen and are ready for their awakening, to be able to join others who await them. Remember to drink the water, child, before sitting and before eating. This will be your first sitting for a very long time (*had not participated in rescue work since we sat with Ruth and Leslie Bone*), you will receive healing when all has been completed.

'Yeha Noha.'

We duly sat the next evening, following all White Feather's instructions to the letter. We had a very successful rescue circle and, with the help of our friends in Spirit, were able to send these two lost souls on to their family and friends who were waiting for them. We recorded these whilst they were taking place and have kept them. To date we have a number of recordings of our rescue work. Rescue work to me is so very fulfilling. We usually find that we too shed tears after each one finds their rightful place in Spirit. They are so lost and alone when they first come to us, so unhappy, wondering where they are. I try to put myself in their place, a hard thing to do really as I am still of the Earth, but I try to visualise how I would feel if I suddenly found myself in a situation such as theirs. It must be very frightening and also very frustrating. The only thing that I can liken it to would be, say, to waking up after an accident, perhaps after being in a coma for several days or weeks, and not recognising where you are or even who all the strange faces that surround you belong to, even if those faces are family and friends whom you should recognise.

It is not always sadness and gloom with them; sometimes we have the odd comedian who goes off in fits of laughter when we tell them that they have passed over and now need to be in the Spirit world, until they realise that what we are telling them is the truth. We had one dear old lady who didn't even know what electricity was. They only had candles for light in her days on Earth. She had been gone a very long time, just drifting and wandering aimlessly. I think I mentioned the postman who had collapsed whilst delivering mail. His only concern was that his wife would be worried about his absence at dinner! It is very strange to talk to some of these people, but at the same time it is fascinating. Everyone is different: the only thing that they have in common is that they have left this earth and their physical bodies behind.

Lodge of the White Bear

Shamanic Practitioner

Certificate of Distinction

This is to certify that

Geraldine Pengelly, BSSH

has completed a foundation course in

~ Shamanic Healing ~

a course of Shamanic Training & Personal Development

and is hereby qualified to work as a

Shamanic Practitioner

Signed

Merlynne Whitebear

BSc., DHP, FMANF, BSYA(acu), RI.SPD

Dated: 25th October, 2004

Kerys Laughing Bear

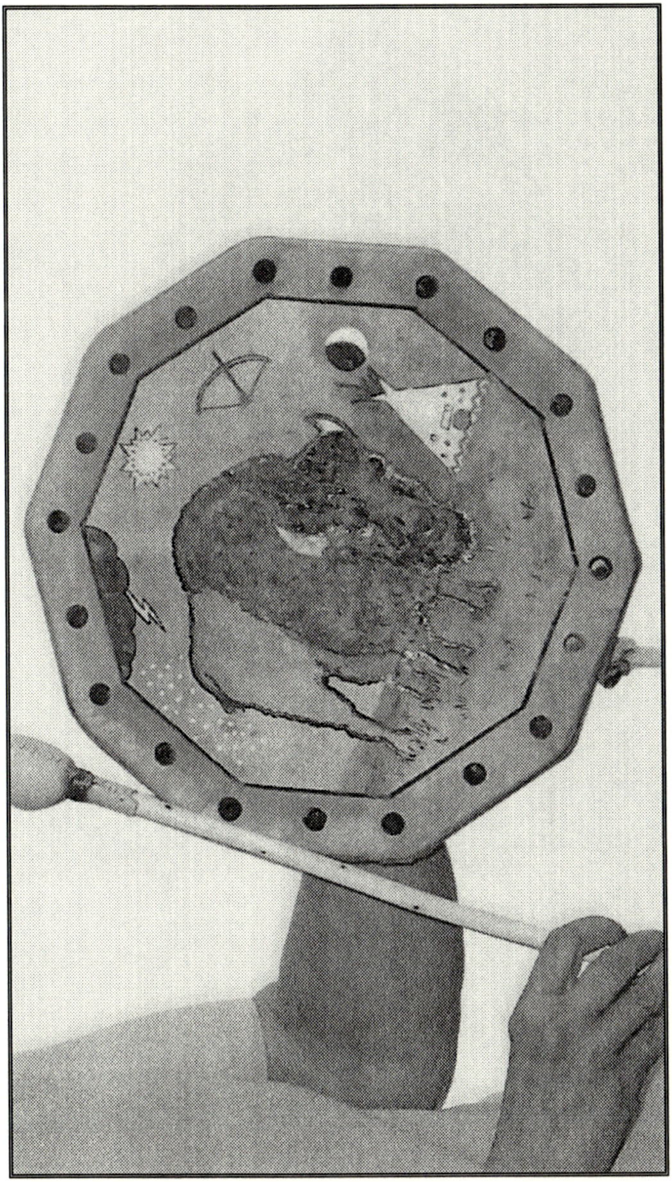

The author's drum

The author's medicine shield

Geraldine, Steve and Gwyn, taken at Harewood Park

Gwyn, Steve and Geraldine at Avebury Circle, summer 2005

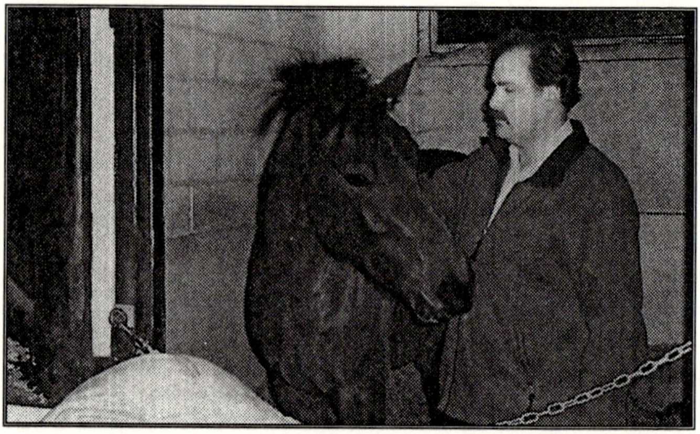

Martin Cox, horse whisperer and animal healer

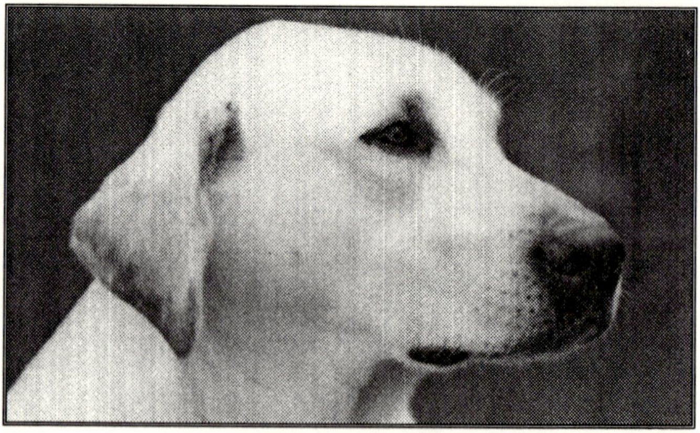

Angus, now in Spirit

Woody

Geraldine and Victor receiving a joint birthday gift

Fox, drawn for the author by Gwyn Cox

Everything Happens for a Reason

It is now three months since I had my first sitting with White Feather. So much has happened to me in this time. I have become more aware of things around me in my daily life and it seems that I have a different perspective on life in general than I had before. My home is filled with a lovely warm, glowing feeling, my energy level has increased and I seem to sail through my daily tasks with ease.

My whole being feels utter contentment. I look forward to my daily conversations with White Feather and answers to questions I have in my thoughts are quickly answered.

Having said this, however, I am now going to contradict myself. When we are sitting at meditation times, just sitting quietly listening to healing music we have on CD, I find myself mentally acknowledging all that I am being given – i.e. colours, profiles of faces, vibrations etc. – but find myself wondering what, if anything, my husband is receiving. Vic still has trouble clearing his mind when we are sitting for meditation. This puts up what we call barriers. This bothers me, and as a result my own 'openness' to Spirit starts to drop at these times, although I seem to revert to awareness at other times – e.g. during the day and during my nightly dreamtimes. My concentration at our sitting times keep drifting as I wonder what

Vic is receiving. I knew that Abraham (Vic's guide) was trying very hard to connect with him and I just could not understand why it was not happening. The following was given to me a week later.

Tuesday, 8 October

White Feather: 'Come, child, we go to the lake to speak of matters that concern you and to free yourself of thoughts that cloud your consciousness.' I sat and listened to the music being played very softly and then the rhythm of the drum began. I felt myself floating above the room, rising higher and higher. Once again I felt the wind in my face and then the feeling of coming back down until my feet rested on soft grass.

White Feather was standing at the edge of the lake. He motioned to me to sit on the log while he remained standing. After what seemed like ages, he spoke.

'There is no need to concern yourself, child: we know of your thoughts and would say to you, Do not relive the problems of the past few yesterwhiles (*this is White Feather's word for yesterday, or even a month or two ago*). Do not let thoughts of self-doubt descend upon you: we are aware of all. We bring light and love and would ask that you think of the light of the Great Spirit surrounding you; think of his love and light as a cloak covering your entirety. Fill your thoughts with the beauty of the flowers, the trees and all you see. Breathe in the scent of the flowers and listen to the song of the birds as they sing to you. Think happy thoughts, child, and all will be as it should be. There is a new development ahead of you, Sehywha: this will come by way of much hard work, studying etc., but will also be one of great enjoyment.

Laughing Bear has recognised the potential within you and has words of advice for you. Listen to him, child.

'Our dear friend Abraham gives his thoughts of love to you and thanks you for being his instrument to speak with his friend Mon Ami. He knows of your concerns and he calls it "the desire to run before you can walk syndrome". Patience in all things is the way we learn and go forward, one step at a time. Impatience causes the wrong things to happen at the wrong time. When thoughts are heard, stop and let the thoughts move closer to you. It will then give the bigger picture of what is being given to you. Now, my child, let all thoughts of concern leave you. Let them rest here where it is so peaceful and let your soul be filled with the beauty of all around you. Do not be anxious about your Earth daughter, for by noon you will hear that all is well. We shall keep her safe. (*This concerned my daughter, Lesley, who had had a minor operation on her bladder and had spent the previous day and night in hospital.*) Remember our earlier quiet moments, when we spoke of how much one prayer to Spirit means. Let your heart be filled with love, send your thoughts to all who are in need. Remember to drink the water, child. We shall speak again soon.

'Yeha Noha.'

(*P.S. to this morning's sessions: Lesley rang at 11.15 a.m. to say that all is well. She is a bit tired and did not sleep last night: she had a nosebleed caused by the tubes they put up her nose. She is going to bed to sleep.*)

I duly sent my thoughts of love and thanks to White Feather and Spirit for Lesley's recovery and for the phone call.

Wednesday, 9 October

Felt better this morning; slept quite well last night. White Feather: 'We are here, child. Do not do anything other than that of necessity for this day. Do not concern yourself with the thoughts of others and the words they speak. We have spoken before about negativity, have we not? You, child, are well protected, wearing the cloak of the Great Spirit's love and golden light. Do not let others decide what is right for you: you are a free Spirit and as such should follow your own counsel and the path you yourself have chosen. Stay on this path, Sehywha: it is the right path for you. There are others who question what you do, but do not listen to them. They do not know you or the unique gift that is yours. We have waited a very long time to show ourselves to you, now you see us and know that what you feel, hear and see is the truth. As we have said before, child, you are not a fortune-teller: your ability goes far beyond that. You will recognise those that believe in what you do, for you have the "soul's eye" to see what lies beyond the face that is shown to the world (*will explain more about this at the end of this teaching*). Keep your heart light, my child, and let your thoughts be filled with love and all the beautiful places you have seen. Take time to listen to your music, read the many books you have acquired concerning Spirit. The more you learn the easier is the path to full and complete understanding.

'It matters not that others find you, in their words, "strange" because you do not seek their company. There are many who do not have the ability to live the quiet life. You do, child: you know that you are not alone, for are we not with you always? Others who do not have the knowledge of Spirit suggest you should do this or that or go here or there. This causes conflict within you because you wish to be left alone to follow your own routine. We have spoken before, have we not, about the times when your path would be rocky, and the other times when it would be smooth? We would say to you, my dear child, Keep your vision, for you have a goal. Do not listen to those who say they have your best interests at heart. Listen to your inner self, Sehywha, for did not the Great Spirit teach us, To your own self be true?

'Enough for this time, my child. We shall be here, and when you sit in the quiet at sunset, we will show you more of the path you tread toward your true golden goal. Do not forget the water. Rest well.

'Yeha Noha.'

A little explanation about the 'face beneath'. It is quite hard to explain, but I will try. When you look at a person's face normally, it shows you what it wants you to see, the face they show the world. When I look at a person, I see the normal face and then when I look deeper, what I call looking at them with my third eye, I see another face. The best explanation for this is, if a person is lying to you or only appearing to be friendly when they actually feel differently, by looking deeper I can see the true face underneath the falsity. This is not the smiling image they show outwardly, but an ugly, twisted and contorted one. This then tells me to use my shield or put my guard up so that I have protection against any negative energy that is around. Perhaps the expression 'two-faced' came about because of this.

Wednesday, continued

I was about to go and have a shower when I was asked to

sit with my book. Strange vibration: not White Feather. I heard a voice and then recognised Abraham.

'Hello, Lady, my friend White Feather has given permission for me to speak to you for a short while. We understand you are rebuilding your energy levels so we cannot speak thro' you at present. We thank you for your help with Mon Ami (*Vic*). He is struggling at present. Matters do not move quickly enough for him. There is much we wish to share with him to assist him with his true work, but until he sits in the quiet he cannot hear us. There is just one message for him at present and it is this: "Hello, Mon Ami, Spirit wishes to work with you and through you. You are known to us as the 'healer of the mind': the one who helps others to release the anxieties and thoughts that may prevent them living their everyday lives. To this end, Mon Ami, you study hard: we will help you. When you speak of your achievements to others it should be done quietly and not for praise of the ego. The lady may not know your every thought, but we do. Mon Ami, listen to the lady: she is the person who will help you on your journey through this mortal life. If all goes well, it will be the last time you make this journey (*it appears that Vic has been here before and has led a few infamous lives and has been told by his guide that he could not tell him of some of the things he has done in his past lives*). Your progression to higher planes depends on what you have learned whilst here this time. When you sit with the lady at sunset we will be with you, to show images of what lies ahead. There will be good things and many happy times. Consider all that this one has said. Au revoir." '

I feel I am finished now: all energy has gone. I felt Abraham's presence very strongly whilst he was speaking and now he has gone I feel quite limp. A nice shower and something to eat should bring me back to par!

Whilst I was having my meal I thought about what Abraham had said. I read and re-read his message to my husband and hoped that when he read it when he came home from work he would understand everything that Abraham had spoken of.

Monday, 14 October

This is in answer to my apology to White Feather for missing three days' sittings and writings in my book due to a bad cold. I did not feel that I would be receptive to Spirit whilst feeling 'one degree under'.

White Feather: 'Do not concern yourself, child, about the times you do not write my words. You know we are very close to you and see all. We will talk: you can hear. If you do not write the words, no matter: questions will come again when you are able to write the answers. Our friend Abraham is pleased with the work that is growing with Mon Ami. He is saying that the learning will become easier because the knowledge is being given strongly. Abraham suggests that when you next sit at sunset, Mon Ami, after making himself comfortable, should think of his guide and of nothing else. Abraham wishes to speak with him directly and, if the vibrations are as one, then he will hear him and the words he speaks.

'Now, my dear child, we leave you to your work. Rest well after your tasks and be sure to drink the water. We see busy times ahead for you with the work you do for Spirit. Remember, Sehywha, your work for Spirit does not go unnoticed. In return you will find your gift growing and sight, sound and inner vision becoming much clearer. Listen to all you hear and look well at all you see with both inner and outer vision. Feel the energy that is all around you and recognise what that feeling is.

'Yeha Noha.'

It would seem that my husband has become a little more aware since he read Abraham's message. He feels that he wants, more than anything else, to hear Abraham's voice speaking to him directly. He admits that he is impatient at times and wants everything yesterday, so to speak. But he realises that this is not going to happen. He has to slow his thinking down and do as Abraham has told him to do. Once he is 'in tune' with Abraham I feel he will fly.

Thursday, 15 October

White Feather: 'Thank you, child, for hearing our call to sit. Sit quietly, Sehywha, and let all thoughts drift away. We will go to the lake and speak of things to come.' I sat quietly, relaxed, listened to the gentle music I could hear and breathed with the beat of the drum. I found myself floating, travelling through the air, my body completely weightless.

My feet are touching the soft grass and I know without opening my eyes that we are at the lake. I open my eyes and look around me. No matter how many times I see this place I still feel overcome by the sheer beauty, the peace and the feelings of love all around me. We sit by the water, White Feather on the ground and I on the log, in what I can only describe as comfortable and harmonious silence. After a while White Feather speaks: 'It is noted that the writings go well, child. Remember to write as you see: mind every little detail, see the picture as a whole, not in part. These writings will help in your future. Indeed, you could not have a better learning tool. We are slowly building up the energies of your lodge (*home*); they grow stronger. But you know this, Sehywha; we do not have to speak the words. We wish to speak about the dangers of persuasion. There are those who say they have your best interests at heart and will try to make you say or do what you feel is not right for you. Listen to your inner thoughts, child: do not pull against your true feelings. Listen to the many voices that speak to you and learn the difference between truth and falsehood. You can already see the face beneath the smile: now recognise the voice. Listen to the tone and for the answer that comes too quickly, when the question has barely been asked. You may also feel the "falsehood"; this comes to you as a wall of coldness. We do not say to judge every word you hear, only those few that would drain your energy and bring sadness to you. We have spoken before, have we not, about sensitivity? Child, the gift that you have is precious and will bring you much joy. It must also be said that it can bring unrest, because you see the truth. The truth sometimes hurts, Sehywha, but if you remember all we have spoken of and the learning you hold deep inside you, you will overcome all that comes before you. Remember the lion, his strength. Remember also to use your shield, child. It is there for you to place between yourself and matters that cannot be rectified. Unfortunately there are those who cannot be helped: they cannot see that the answers to their problems lie within themselves.

'For those people, the earth life is like climbing a mountain each day of their lives. Their burdens are many and as such bring a heaviness that they feel they must carry. Only when Spirit is recognised for what it offers – beauty, peace, and above all else love for one and all – will the beauty of the soul emerge and give the untold joy that is Spirit. You, my child, are truly blessed with the knowledge of Spirit and therefore know that all we say is true.'

White Feather squats down and puts his hand into the water and makes ripples that spread over the surface of the lake. When the water is still again he speaks: 'Look at what you see, child, and keep this image within you. This is your destiny, toward which you tread the path. (*I seem to be in a large room or hall. There are people, so many faces looking at me. I am speaking but cannot hear the words; I can only see my mouth and know that the words are being spoken. I am so happy I feel like crying. I can feel myself talking, going on and on. It is not possible to describe the emotions going through me. I am alone, standing on a box or something similar. I am alone but not alone. Sounds rubbish, but I cannot explain this feeling.*) White Feather: 'This is your total achievement, child: keep this image and mind what has been shown. You have much to do, Sehywha, and your reward for this will be the exact feelings you had when you looked into the water. We know that you will embrace all that comes to you. Even we have moments when we feel emotion. We too feel the happiness that brings tears of pure joy.

'Enough for this time, child. We will speak again soon. Keep the image and the feelings you have at this time and take it with you. Think of the happy times to come. As always, rest well and take the water.

'Yeha Noha.'

This is the longest time I have spent with White Feather:

we seem to get closer each time we speak. I even felt his emotion this time! I also feel his love and his kindness. I pray that when it is my time to leave this life, he will be the one who comes to escort me home.

Wednesday, 16 October

Vic and I sat this evening for development. Much was given to me: faces, bright colours. At one stage the energy built up so much that bright disks were all around the room. Towards the end of the sitting Vic saw part of Abraham's face and his late father's image. Vic also felt something touch his arm and said he knew it was Spirit and not his imagination. Just before we closed our sitting, White Feather came through me, singing. We listened to the tape recording after we had finished and closed our circle and could not make out the words. It sounded like his own language, Shoshoni. We did hear the words 'Yeha Noha'. Vic and I discussed what we had been given during our sitting. Vic said he had seen his nan and granddad (now in Spirit) and the house they had lived in when they were here. The next thing I am going to tell you about explains why I do not believe in coincidence and only that everything happens for a reason.

The following weekend, whilst clearing out his shed, Vic found some old music tapes we had put there during one of our many clear-outs. We decided to play them, just to see if they were worth keeping. One of the tapes was titled *Pure Moods* with various artists. One of the tracks was called 'Yeha Noha – Wishes of Happiness and Health'. Well, when we played it my husband's and my jaws dropped. It was the same song White Feather had sung at our sitting the previous Wednesday. Another treasure Vic unearthed was an old tin box and inside was a very old photograph of his nan and granddad standing at the gate leading to their house. What lucky finds! As I said before, I don't believe in coincidence. The sitting, the song and the image that Vic had of his grandparents were, in my opinion, a thank you from Spirit. We will treasure it always. This box had been in our shed for at least eight years. Vic had, prior to our sitting, been looking for this photograph as it was the only one he had of his nan and granddad. That was his thank you. The song 'Yeha Noha' was a gift to me, I feel, from White Feather. Now I understand his closing words at the end of each lesson.

Monday, 21 October

Did not sit this morning, sat in the afternoon after I had rested from my chores.

I heard White Feather chuckling to himself as he came through. He said he had been teaching Abraham an old tribal dance used for celebrations and special occasions. The reason for the laughter was that Abraham could not tell his left from his right.

White Feather: 'We must apologise for our chanting, Sehywha: it did not sound as we intended, but we think you recognised what was being said. We were very happy that you were able to verify this with your find. We hope to give more of our natural tongue in the future. We have many messages of love to give you, child, and to Mon Ami also. Many friends, together with family, bring their love and wishes of happiness to you both. They also see the advancement you have made with the work for Spirit. The message for Mon Ami from his earth father is, in his words, "It's about time you found yourself a job you really enjoy. If you stick at it you will get the benefit of helping others as well as yourself. When you get qualified, remember to frame your certificate and hang it for all to see. Fancy that: my son learning a trade at last. I know that some pieces of paper mean very little but this one you should be very proud of. You know me, I don't say much: but just because I don't speak doesn't mean I am not interested in what is going on. I hope to be at one of your 'sessions' when you get going. By the way, it doesn't matter whether you work where you are now or a few counties away: I can still make it." ' White Feather resumed: 'We hope we have interpreted the father's message in the right way: the main feeling coming here is love. With all the help our friend is receiving from Spirit, Abraham is saying: "It is a walk in the park." Press on, Mon Ami. Do not give up on your search for lost or mislaid items. They do have a way of being found.'

The message for Vic from his dad was simply that at last Vic had a qualification and a job that he enjoyed (hypnotherapy). When Vic's Dad, Ben, was alive he had tried in every way to persuade Vic to get a degree in engineering, but at the time Vic said he was not interested and that it would mean too much studying. Now, after completing his hypnotherapy course, which included lots and lots of studying, he had the qualification that allowed him to become a 'healer of minds'. We are both absolutely over the moon!

Tuesday, 22 October

I thanked White Feather for those on our healing list who were being healed, especially for Beccy and her baby. White Feather: 'We are happy that all goes well, child, and would say that the prayers for healing are indeed heard. It is because there is the thought for others together with the wish to help those in need of Spiritual healing that it is possible. Of course, my child, there are times when Spirit cannot help. This would be the time for that one to pass to Spirit. Some things are hard to explain to you, Sehywha: you can only understand what you call "the process" when you yourself are in Spirit. Best for you now to accept what you do not understand, continue with your prayers, and put your trust in Spirit.

'To future matters, now. The next sitting time for yourself and Mon Ami should be concentrated again on sound. Abraham wishes to communicate directly with Mon Ami. Abraham tells me that the channel should be clearer now that old debris has been removed. If the feelings of tiredness should overcome you, give in to them: Abraham's voice will still be heard. We wish to use your energy for this, Sehywha. Keep your thoughts inside the lodge. If it helps to keep yourself in focus, concentrate on Abraham's image. Think how pleased our friend will be once contact is made. Once Abraham's voice is heard communication can be made on many occasions. They will learn to speak as we do, Sehywha, and with the same frequency.

'One other event we wish to speak of, child, and it is this. Because of matters that will arise in the future, we have a new addition to the voice box. You already know of him, Sehywha: he will be your gatekeeper for those who have messages for family and friends. You will call him Jacky. As already told to you, he is known to you and will be a valuable tool for you to work with. It is easier for him to be your contact whilst working with Spirit because his level is not too much above your own. For obvious reasons, this one (*White Feather*) cannot be used for long periods of time. It would take too much energy and very little of the message would be able to be given. We know you understand this, child, so will not dwell on it any longer. You may use the music when you next sit with Mon Ami; this helps him to relax. Rest now, child, for whilst so doing we replenish the energy used this time.

'Yeha Noha.'

Thursday, 24 October

Just a short message from White Feather today to say, 'No writings this time, child, we will not take too much energy. We wish to say that we are more than pleased with the sitting you did together. We make good progress.

'Yeha Noha.'

Monday, 28 October

This sitting is given over to Abraham, who wishes to say a few things to Vic. Abraham: 'Hello, Lady, thank you for hearing me. We wish to say to Mon Ami: You progress well, my friend. We are pleased with your inner view of clarity. It is so important for you to be able to define each item as it is given. The brightness of colour too will be of great benefit to you, when you are asked for definitions of exactness. There is so much beauty to see if one cares to take the time to appreciate. Now you have mastered how to meditate we will be able to give you much more. (We have to calm ourselves so that we give the lady our message to you. We get too excited at our plans for you and we are told to go slowly so that she may write.) We have many, many plans for you, Mon Ami, and look forward to travelling the path of Light with you. In time,

Mon Ami, you too, like the lady, will hear, see and feel all that is given. We are with you constantly and thank you for sending your thoughts to us. There is no need for you to fear anything, Mon Ami. We are protecting you. No harm will befall you: you are in safe hands. When fearful thoughts come to you, just say the magic words: "I have my guide, Abraham, and his protection all around me. Nothing can cause me harm." The fearful thought will then fade into nothingness. In time, Mon Ami, you will fear nothing at all. We are eager to begin working with you and would say to you, Be prepared for even more to come, the next time you sit with the lady. We will now say Au revoir.'

I was about to put my book away when White Feather came: 'Thank you, my child, for being so patient with our friend (*Abraham*). He sometimes gets too excited and has to be reminded to take time to settle himself. However, we are all different in our vibrations and no doubt he views me as somewhat severe in my manner. Little does he know that I too have my softer moments and have known many sad occasions when, had it been possible for tears to flow, they would have. Enough for this time, my dear child. We shall speak again soon.

'Yeha Noha.'

I feel very honoured and privileged that Abraham speaks through me and to me. I feel very different when I write words from Abraham: he is quite jovial in his manner and very mischievous. He also giggles a lot. When he gets excited, his words come very quickly but I can understand what he is telling me. He is a very dear soul who has a great deal of knowledge he wishes to pass on to Vic in his capacity as teacher.

Tuesday, 29 October

Felt the need to rise earlier today and sit. Saw White Feather in what looked like a large soap bubble floating about five feet from the ceiling. He went around the room, out into the kitchen, back into the lounge and finally came to rest on the floor in front of my chair. He lifted one arm and began to sing/chant (could not understand the words he sang). He told me to look at this right hand that was lifted, palm facing me. His palm became bigger and bigger until it took on the dimension of a TV screen. Pictures of different things began appearing on this screen. He showed me a North American Indian, similar to himself but younger, no feathers, just a band around his head. He had long black hair with a centre parting. He wore nothing above the waist, just necklaces of many colours, and ribbons of red and orange tied to the top of his arms. He held what looked like a club with ribbons at the handle end. He wore suede trousers edged with braiding and soft suede slipper-like shoes on his feet.

White Feather finished his song/chant and spoke: 'Sehywha, this is your third guide. His name is Little Elk, and he also has another name, James Lone Elk. His work with you is as a clearer. He will go ahead of you, sweeping all obstacles away and making sure that the pathways are free from debris so that nothing interferes with the thought. This will make the channels clearer and communication stronger.'

The picture changed to show another man, again naked from the waist up, wearing satin or silk cream-coloured trousers that looked like very large bloomers. He wore nothing on his feet, and had a black sash tied at his waist. He was olive-skinned, completely bald, and had one gold earring in his left ear. I noticed his very black eyes and how they seemed to shine. He had very full red lips also. He was smiling at me and nodding.

White Feather: 'There is no need to name this one, child. You already know him by name but this is the first time you have seen his image.' (*I knew instantly that this was the Egyptian, Houssain, who a medium at our local church had said appeared to be hovering around me.*) White Feather continued: 'This lovely soul is your protector, Sehywha: we have been told to say the word "bodyguard", which you will understand better. He places himself between you and any threat to you, be it word or deed.' White Feather stood up and came towards me, so close that I could feel a tingling go right through me. 'Rest now, child, let all thoughts of concern float away, and think of the lake and all the beauty you have seen. Sleep and rest easy. We are with you: you are not alone.' I felt him blow in my face and then he was gone. I heard his voice from a distance saying 'Sweet dreams' and then 'Yeha Noha'.

There was no way I was going to 'rest easy', as he put it – not after all that! So now it would seem two other guides have been assigned to me. Both appear to have different work to do. I remember that a very long time ago I was told that I had four guides. Well, I now know three; one more to be shown to me. I expect it will come in time, I do not ask or question. Everything is done for a reason.

On the following Friday (1 November) I was getting ready for my weekly shopping trip to town when I heard White Feather's voice calling me, so I sat and waited for the connection. 'Do not walk thro' the park today, Sehywha, take the longer path,' was all he said. I decided to take a taxi to town instead of taking the bus. I usually go by bus to the bus station and then take a short cut through the park to the shops. The taxi would drop me in the actual shopping area.

I told my husband about this mystery message when he got home from work later that day, and he said he wondered why I had been told not to walk through the park.

Just as I was getting ready for bed I heard White Feather asking me to sit and write. His message was for Vic: 'Nothing happened in the park, my friend, because Sehywha was not there. If there comes a time when we can help to prevent certain matters, we will do so.'

That was it, nothing else. It looked, said Vic, as if I could have been mugged or something similar. Just to verify what White Feather had said, we scanned the local paper the next day looking for something that might have happened in the park, but could not find anything.

Before I continue with our next lesson I wish to once again 'set the scene' so you understand White Feather's messages. Last Christmas Vic gave me an electric organ. I had a few lessons from a music teacher who lived locally and was steaming ahead with my music. I love music, anything that is soothing, and many of my music books were of shows such as *Phantom of the Opera*, *Miss Saigon*, etc. Because of this, I had to spend time practising each day, and I began to get a little worried that I was not spending enough time listening for While Feather's call to our other lessons. I mentally apologised to him for this and told myself that I would get up early the next day and sit ready with my book for White Feather's visit.

Tuesday, 5 November

As soon as Vic had left for work I got up and sat with my

book ready for White Feather. I did not have to wait long as he came through very clear and very loud. 'We wish to speak about our talks, child. We understand your concern, and would say to you, Do not worry. We approve of your love for music and that much time must be given to the learning of the instrument so that you may play with ease. We have no wish to interfere with your earthly living or with the pleasure that you find in your music. As we have spoken before, child, we shall be here for you when you feel the need to talk with us. Do not feel that you have to sit each day; if there is anything we wish to say to you we shall choose a time that does not interfere with your daily workings. You have many talents, child; we watch and see what you do. Your time is always spent giving, asking nothing for yourself. Indeed, we know you wish that there were more time to do everything you want to do. Unfortunately we cannot help with this; we cannot give more time or stretch the time you have to fit everything into your earthly life. We wish we could. We can, however, help you glide through busy times so that they go smoothly. Just take the time for your meditation, this is important. This helps with channelling and our connection. Your music will give you relaxation and comfort. Do not try so hard, child; as with your meditation let yourself feel what is inside. Take your time to think about your day. When you rise, think about the time ahead and plan your day. We know it is not always possible for matters to go exactly as you would wish, but for most of the time they will. There will be times, child, when we need to speak of matters that you must know; these will be given, as always, with your best interests in mind. When you feel the need to boost your energies, Sehywha, go to the mountains and the lake and let yourself be filled with all that you see there. We shall be there for you and we will talk. We have a bond between us, child, and thus there are times when talk is not needed. There is also another sign that your development grows in momentum. You are beginning to talk to me with your inner voice. We hear you without watching the lip movement. This is how we communicate in Spirit, Sehywha.

'Your inner being tells you when matters do not go well. You are understanding most things now, child. There is also something that you have yet to realise: you can now give words of wisdom to all who seek your company. People who know you will speak of many things and will look to you to give them verification of what they seek. Strangers will feel the need to speak to you, perhaps about trivial matters. Listen to all, child: they all have a meaning in your earthly life. Ask for guidance with the silent tongue. We will answer your questions. All goes well, child, with the prayers for healing and help for those travelling in the darkness. When next you sit with Mon Ami, both Abraham and myself will be present. Rest well now, child, and do not forget the water.

'Yeha Noha.'

From this lesson it would appear that White Feather will call me when he has something important to say to me. He is right when he says that I wish there were more hours in the day. I cannot remember just how many times I have said this over the last few years. Even though I am now at home every day I still cannot find time to fit everything in. Heaven only knows how I found time to work full-time, as well! I try to make myself a list each day of chores to be done – i.e. washing, ironing, cleaning, shopping etc. – and try to fit my other pursuits around these. Luckily I only need to cook once a day, our evening meal, so that saves a little time. To write this book, taking all our daily, weekly talks from my working books, has taken one full day per week of typing. This is where my husband's help has been such a blessing: he takes over, making me drinks and getting the meals so I can get my typing done. Thank you, Vic.

Tuesday, 12 November

I tried sitting earlier today, but nothing happened so I got on with my chores. I heard White Feather say, 'Later, Sehywha.'

It was nearly lunchtime when I heard him asking me to sit. White Feather: 'Come, child. We will visit the mountains and the lake, breathe the fresh mountain air and drink in the beauty of all we see and hear.' Today's experience of travelling seemed to be different. I did not feel the movement of actually going anywhere, just a peaceful, floating feeling.

The mountains come into view first, like a sunrise. They grow bigger and the whole view grows wider to include the lake, until the whole of the picture is complete. This must be the most perfect place there can be. If there is such a place as paradise then this must be it. Nowhere on earth could be compared to the scene I am looking at now. Everywhere is calm and peaceful and very still.

White Feather is there, sitting by the lake. He motions me to sit alongside him. 'You understand now, child, that you can come here at any time you wish: peace and tranquillity are just a thought away. During your busy times you will think of this place and know that when you have completed your chores you will be able to replenish your strength at this, your special place. As your energy levels rise, you will be able to "travel" more quickly and more often. When you use your energy for Spirit, child, as you do, you must replace what you use, thus maintaining the same steady flow and enabling even more awareness than you have at present.

We speak enough this time, child. We shall leave you to enjoy what you can now call your retreat. We shall speak again soon. Rest well, Sehywha. Remember the water.

'Yeha Noha.'

I sat for quite a while after I had 'returned' from my visit to the mountains and the lake, feeling like a child who has been given a bag of sweets. How wonderful: I can go to this lovely place whenever I feel the need! But I must not get carried away or I will end up spending all my time here, and that would never do: I have my earthly life to live. I will keep my visits to a minimum, only going when I need to. That way I will feel it is a treat.

Before I write the next lesson from White Feather I feel a little more explanation is necessary so that you fully understand what his messages mean. As I told you before, my husband has a problem with just sitting still for any length of time. He has difficulty in just relaxing and letting go of all his thoughts. He also feels very disappointed when Spirit does not speak through me whilst we are sitting in circle. Unfortunately he has a tendency to voice these thoughts and when he does, usually White Feather will give me a message for him, or as my husband puts it, 'a telling off'. Having said this, the following should make sense to you.

Thursday, 28 November

Heard White Feather asking me to sit so that explanations could be given regarding last night's circle. White Feather: 'My child, we wish to speak of sitting with Mon Ami. We have spoken of this before but feel further words are necessary so that he fully understands the message given. It takes much energy to be used for voice. The energies that are being built in your lodge are growing. We do not want to take away what is being given at present (*energy*). The sittings are to enable us to give images, colours and sounds. The purpose of such is so that when the time is right you will recognise immediately what is being given, to open the channels of sight and sound. We hear the word "disappointed". Why? There is much being given to you and what is being given is very precious and should be recognised as such. The whole concept of what is being given is for the purpose of understanding the world of Spirit. We hear "I've been told off again." We do not want you to take what is being said as a reprimand. It is not. It is to help you see that the whole purpose of what you are doing at present is to build toward an eventual goal. This goal will take the form of messages from Spirit to those seeking answers from the Spirit world. When you sit you are working although you do not always think you have received anything. We can assure you that there is much being given to you. Because you already know the way of the Spirit, Sehywha, we do not have to explain to you. Our advice to Mon Ami is for him to read the writings already recommended (*books White Feather had mentioned in one of our earlier circles, in particular one on meditation*). This will help him to understand the ways of Spirit. He knows that to achieve the whole knowledge of his subject (*hypnotherapy*) and to fulfil his goal – a paper on which his name is written – will take much reading and understanding. We do not give him a paper, but what will be given will be even more precious. Mon Ami needs much encouragement to slow down and take time to enjoy each moment whilst sitting. He should be aware that Abraham is working very hard to bring him his gifts of sight and sound. We have a message for Mon Ami from his earth father and it is this: "Think back to your teenage years and what we spoke about. I told you that there was nothing you could not do if you put your mind to it. I want to say it again now. Be patient and listen to what is being said to you. I do not have to tell you how important this is going to be for everyone, yourself included. I too have had to learn and am still learning now!" ' 'White Feather continues: 'Our final thought to end this sitting is that the word of the moment is "patience". As we have said before, child, a tree does not grow overnight; it needs time to be nourished to grow tall and straight. The nourishment for you is being given each time you sit in circle. Speak with Mon Ami, tell him to keep his channels open to receive what is being sent. Rest now, child.

'Yeha Noha.'

Tuesday, 10 December

This is the first opportunity I have had to sit since the last circle.

White Feather: 'Do not feel sad, child, because you have not written. We communicate and do not need the paper. The writings are your working tool for what may arise at some time in the future.

'We shall go home today, Sehywha. We will show you

our people and our lodges. Close your eyes, child, listen to the beat of the drum, breathe in time with that beat.'

I did as White Feather said. I heard the drum very softly at first. Then it began to get louder. I heard White Feather telling me to clear all thoughts away except for his voice.

'We have a very long way to go, child. Just free your thoughts of everything else and feel the cloak of love that surrounds you.' I felt myself floating upward and then I was going forward very fast. We seemed to travel through darkness and then light. I could feel the wind rushing past my face and still we went on. I began to think the journey would never end, but it did.

'Open your eyes, child. Welcome to our home.' I am standing on a hilltop of green grass and, looking down, I see a sea of tepees. Many people: men, women and children. We begin to walk down the hill towards the village. The people I see are all Indian, no white person in sight. As we reach the village the people come towards me, smiling and holding out their arms to me. White Feather: 'Come, child, you are expected.' We walk through the crowd of people. They do not speak but their thoughts say, Welcome. I feel many hands touching me and feel very comfortable and very happy. I feel the children holding my hands, and every so often more come. They are hanging on to my clothes. Every face is smiling and happy. Everyone is colourful, some wearing traditional dress and others bright ribbons and feathers in their hair. Some hair is straight, some is braided.

We stop at the first tepee. Standing outside is a very elderly man with a very colourful headdress. He has a lovely smile and his eyes twinkle. He holds both my hands and shakes them several times, then gestured to me to enter his lodge. This is White Feather's father – don't ask me how I know this: I just do. Inside the lodge it is very warm, and I am surprised at how big it is. I am asked to sit on what looks like a fur bundle. I sit next to White Feather and his father sits opposite. A woman comes into the lodge and I immediately know that she is White Feather's mother. (After I acknowledge this fact in my mind I look at White Feather and see he is nodding at me.)

The next person who comes into the lodge is a very small lady with a beautiful smile and a lovely face. The name Morning Star comes into my thoughts. (Once again I know that White Feather is nodding his approval.) Three young men complete our circle around the centre of the lodge. Two are quite tall, while the third one is shorter and much stockier. The names that come to my thoughts are Grey Wolf, White Cloud and Little Dog.

They all make me feel very welcome. The lodge is cosy and very light. It has a lovely warm atmosphere. I can hear singing coming from outside. It is a very strange feeling that I am experiencing, I feel very comfortable and at ease even though I didn't know these people but, at the same time, I felt I have known them all my life. Very strange: it is so hard to actually put my feelings down on paper. It wasn't just being there, but all the different smells I was getting as well!

We went outside to watch the dancing that had begun. There was a very festive feeling, like that of a party. The children were playing something similar to 'ring of roses'. There was a great deal of laughter and a sense of everyone being very happy. I was invited to join the dancing and at first I felt very awkward, but they held my hands and showed me how to do the steps, and soon I was really enjoying myself. When the dancing stopped we all sat down in a heap, laughing so much we were almost crying.

White Feather: 'Time to leave now, Sehywha. Do not be sad, we shall return.' I said my goodbyes and there were lots of hugs as I thanked them all for making me feel so welcome. Morning Star held my hand then touched my cheek: her eyes were very misty when she looked at me. Before the emotion got to be too much I felt White Feather guiding me away, saying, 'Now you have met those who also watch over you. Understanding of all you have seen is another part of the whole picture. Now, my child, you must rest and regain your strength. You need to drink much water and keep yourself warm, Sehywha. We shall be with you when next you sit with Mon Ami.

'Yeha Noha.'

I'm back! What an experience! If I thought all the other journeys with White Feather were fantastic, what could I say about this one, except: *Wow*, *wow* and *wow!*

I sat thinking about all the rough periods in my life, days long ago when I just drifted from one situation to another, never having heard about or even given a thought to Spiritual matters. Sometimes I feel that I am two different people, living two different lives. Each time I journey with White Feather I want more and more of all these wonderful places. It is very hard to keep your feet on the ground after experiencing something like this last journey. One of the most striking thoughts I had was how much I felt 'at home' with the people I met and the situation in general. As my grandson would say, 'Spooky!'

I think that this journey with White Feather has got to

be the most memorable. Even now, after three years have passed and after I have gone on so many other visits, the memory of that one is just as vivid.

My learning continued daily. Sometimes we just talked; other times we would visit the lake and the mountains and just sit in silence and look at the beautiful scenery. On one occasion White Feather said, 'Come, child, tell me of your thoughts and dreams.' I thought to myself. Why does he ask? He already knows. 'The answer to this thought, Sehywha, is that I need to hear your interpretation of what you have seen, and by talking you will know the answer. Is it not better to speak face to face? You will then see that the answers given are indeed true. Why should this one mislead you? It is good that you have made contact with Laughing Bear: he will be precise in all that he tells you. Make sure you heed his words, child. As you will discover in the fullness of time, he will be of great comfort to you, both in the words he speaks and in what he shows you.' White Feather started to laugh here, and his laughter grew louder and louder. After a while he continued: 'In your language, child, what are the chances of you meeting a full-blooded Red Indian in your century and in your country?' White Feather resumed his 'serious' face: 'Now, child, your dream of climbing a very large rocky hill. This is your climb to higher knowledge, of all matters Spiritual. You are climbing higher and higher. Your fear of looking down in case you fall is to tell you not to look back, go forward to all that awaits you. Many things happen in Earth life for a purpose. Many people who do not have what you have, child, do not see what is being shown them. We know you seek the purpose of these matters. Good. It is very wise to question.' Again White Feather was quiet, watching the water. 'When next you sit, child, we shall show you something new, something to lift your heart. We shall continue with images and sounds at all different times: this is just to make you aware. Enough for this time, child. Know that we are, as always, just a thought away.

'Yeha Noha.'

A few days later Vic and I visited Steve and Gwyn and spent the day with them. In the evening we went to a demonstration of mediumship and healing and Steve did drawings for different people who were there. I had a reading from a very nice Irish gentleman by the name of Mark. Before we started on the reading Mark asked me what I was doing in connection with Red Indians, the reason being that as soon as I had sat down opposite him, he said a whole crowd of Indians had surrounded me. Mark had to ask them to step back so he could concentrate on the reading for me. Most of what Mark told me I already knew, thanks to my guide White Feather. Mark told me that I would be doing a fair bit of studying shortly but not to worry about it as he could see me passing this particular course with flying colours. (This was the shamanic healing course that I had enrolled on, mainly because I needed to know more about the old ways of the Red Indian.)

The next day I felt quite tired since we did not get home until 1 a.m. and, as always when we have been to a Spiritual meeting, sat up talking for quite a while after. White Feather came through quite early, calling me from my sleep. 'Not enough time is being given to yourself, child. You must take time to uplift your Spirit. If the physical body is tired then it follows that the Spirit cannot complete its true function. We suggest that for this day (*today*) you leave chores that are not necessary. Sit, child, we shall sit with you. It is important for all concerned with your well-being that we concentrate on replacing lost energy. We shall sit together, Sehywha, by the lake and the mountains and fill our souls with perfect peace. We shall leave all problems behind and think of only healing ourself. There are plenty of Spirits here waiting to welcome you, to help with your healing. Do not concern yourself with others, child. They have to do what is right for them. Their problems are not your problems: you cannot solve everyone's life pattern for them. They must do this themselves. Sometimes, child, we know that saying nothing at all is very hard. Someone talks about someone else and their lack of caring, seemingly, about one's existence is hurtful to the soul. Their attitude to life is wrong, child, but they have to live their life in their own chosen way. We think you understand the word "blinkered". They see only what they want to see and no amount of words will change their outlook. You must learn to pay no heed to what is being said, child. You have a path to follow and we will tread this path with you at all times. Know that we are there and that you are not alone. It is such that mortal life is complicated and Spirit life is not. Man, in his infinite wisdom, makes his own problems and then blames everyone else for the outcome. Unfortunately, there are those who will never change, but that, my child, is their affair. You must not concern yourself with their ways. Part of your learning, child, is to be able to recognise what you see, acknowledge what you have seen and then move on, ignoring whys and wherefores. You are one of the lucky ones, Sehywha, in as much as you can take yourself away from all around you and see only true beauty and fill your soul with the love of Spirit.

'Now, child, cleanse your body in the running water (*shower*) and let the music you hear whilst so doing cleanse your soul and mind. We know that you will feel refreshed. For the rest of this day spend your time quietly. No thought is to be given to anything except Spirit. The time spent this way will uplift your soul. Do not take into yourself the thoughts of others and their life matters: this will undo all we wish to give you. Do not allow others to give their worries to you. Tell them politely that you know of their concerns but you cannot help, and that only they can solve what are their own life's issues. Do not forget to use your shield, child: we know you do not use it enough. It is there for that purpose, to protect and keep out unwanted burdens. Enough for now, child, heed what this one has spoken of, and all will be well and as it should be.

'Yeha Noha.'

This last lesson from White Feather was in response to something that had happened recently with someone who, in her words, called herself 'my friend', but was actually talking about me to others, making mockery of what I believed in and what I was doing. I think you get the picture.

Messages from the Other Side and a Gift from Laughing Bear

A few days later I received a phone call from Kerys Laughing Bear. He had at last managed to make contact with White Feather. Kerys said that White Feather was a 'wily character' and that he had had trouble tracking him down. A letter would follow shortly answering the many questions I had asked about my guide. I already gave you his information earlier in the book, but need to set the scene for my next sitting with White Feather.

Went to the lake today and met White Feather. We talked about recent events (phone call from Kerys Laughing Bear). White Feather said he was very pleased that the connection had been made with Kerys. He was happy that great things would come out of the connection between Kerys and myself. Once again White Feather showed his sense of humour by saying, 'Laughing Bear is very clever, child, we did our best to hide from him but he found the answers he was seeking. This one must be losing his abilities to cover his tracks.' White Feather seemed very jubilant today, he seemed taller and straighter and he kept throwing his hands in the air and doing little dance steps on the spot. After a while he stopped and sat down on the grass. I am totally fascinated by the way he does this, it seems that he crosses one leg in front of the other then squats, ending up cross-legged. I know that if I tried to do this I would fall over! For some reason, I do not know why, today is very different. White Feather, as always, picked up on my thoughts. 'The answer to your question, child, is that we have no need to use our mouth for talking. We use our inner mind: our thoughts are sufficient to ask and answer what is said. You have the knowledge, child: now is the time to use it. Do not concern yourself with what others may think or say. Be true to yourself, fill your thoughts with love, send these thoughts to Spirit and all will be well. Now, Sehywha, someone comes to greet you.'

I looked to where White Feather was pointing and saw Vic's dad, Ben. He looked so well and just like he had stepped out of a bath, all clean and shiny. Ben put his arms around me, hugged me and said, 'Did you bring me a rolly?' (Ben used to roll his own cigarettes when he was here).

White Feather: 'This one will leave you to talk, we shall be close by.' I told Ben I was sorry I had not brought a cigarette for him, but would do so if we met again.

'When Vic sees me in the mirror and thinks it is him, tell him it's not, it is me. He does look a lot like me but he's not as strong. Tell him I was the one blowing in his eyes to wake him up. He sleeps too much. He needs to get up and get going. He is not tired, only thinks he is. Thinks problems go away if he sleeps. There is so much more he could be doing if he puts his mind to it. Tell him to make the effort: it will be worth it. There are so many good things coming but he has to work for it. He shouldn't make the same mistakes I did. He should think about it. We look alike: we even have similar traits. I see in him my three failings: we're both obstinate, lack patience and think we know best! Believe me, I look back on some things I did and feel very sad. That's why I say, Don't do what I did.

Tell Ann (*Vic's sister*) I'm sorry I destroyed all the photographs. It was a stupid thing to do. It would have given you kids a great deal of pleasure going through them, remembering old times. But I was so angry, angry knowing I had so little time left, angry with your mother for leaving me alone. It was done out of pure frustration. Forgive me. Look after your sister: she has more than her fair share of illness and problems. She looked after me well. If it hadn't been for her I would have left a lot sooner. I have to tell you, although it fills me with shame now, that I did think about ending it once and for all and probably would have if not for her. Tell her how proud I am of her, and of what she is doing for the sick. Before you get on your high horse I am proud of you too: do not forget this. Be proud of yourself for what you have achieved. Once your new business takes off (*hypnotherapy*) you won't have time to think, let alone sleep! (*Ha! Ha!*)' Ben looked at me, held my hand in his, and said: 'Now, young lady, you are a bit of a dark horse, you kept all this a secret, didn't you? How do you feel about having a Red Indian for a friend? I was so surprised when I found out. Don't feel left out, I am proud of you too, proud to call you daughter, proud to have you in the family.'

White Feather returned and Ben said: 'I think my time with you is up. See you again soon I hope, don't forget the rolly.' Ben walks away, stops, turns and waves, then he is gone.

White Feather: 'Time to return now, child. Rest well, and drink the water. We shall speak again soon.

'Yeha Noha.'

P.S. As I was leaving I heard Ben's voice: 'Tell Vic he may look like me but he is not as good looking and that I can still give him a thick ear if needs be!'

It was the best and longest conversation I had with Ben. Can't wait till Vic gets in so I can tell him all about it.

Later that evening I gave Vic the messages from his dad and he phoned his sister Ann to give her the message for her. By the end of the phone call all three of us were in tears at the words Dad had given all of us. Confirmation was given to me when Ann told us about the photographs. She had not told anyone in the family that Dad had torn up every single photograph he had, except for those in frames, one of him and Vic's mum and one of Ann's wedding. The rest were put in the dustbin!

My next sitting with White Feather concerned our move to Cornwall. My daughter Lesley has asked us if we would like to move nearer to her and her family. This was suggested some time ago and would take the form of an annexe or extension to their house that they planned to have built in the near future. As this is now still in the pipeline after five years, we are understandably wondering if it is ever going to happen. We were going to Lesley's for a long weekend and had decided to broach the subject again and ask how much longer it would take. The following should explain why we did not broach the subject.

The day before we left for our visit to Cornwall, I heard White Feather asking me to sit. 'Hello, my child, we know that matters concerning your future plans go slowly for you at present. This is your life, child. We cannot interfere with man-made decisions: indeed we would not even if we could. All we say to you is have patience. All will be well in the fullness of time. Now, child, having spoken we are now going to say the opposite to you on one matter – not interference, you understand, but advice. We have spoken before of your plans to live beside the ocean and our advice is thus: when you make the journey to visit your daughter say nothing with regard to future plans that would give cause to heated discussion. We hear Mon Ami say he wants to know where he stands. His place is where he is at the present time, and should be treated as so. We have spoken, child, have we not, about the new lodge and its suitability for both you and Mon Ami? The image is very strong at this moment but we would say to you that one word said in a heated moment could destroy the image for ever. Have patience and wait, child. We hear and would say that plans being made include Mon Ami's work with his project to start here. This will give him time to adapt to his new work. When the time comes, and come it will, he will be in a better position, having gained knowledge of his project and its workings so that he may begin almost at once when your move has been completed. You understand what this one is saying, child? Abraham is saying that he will be at Mon Ami's side when he commences his work to help with the flow (*energy?*).

'Meanwhile, live your daily life and go about your chores with lightness in your step knowing that future times will bring much joy and comfort to you.

'One message for you from your earth father: he asks

why you are not playing your music. He enjoys listening to the music you make when you sit at your instrument. Play for him, child. He asks for one song in particular, we do not know this name: "Charmaine". He is saying you will understand his words.

'Now, child, beware of what lies ahead with your friend (*my best friend had just lost her sister to cancer*), she will need much comfort and love. Be strong and give of yourself what is asked; your strength in Spirit will be of great help to you. We shall leave you now, child. Rest before you start your chores. Do not forget to drink the water, and as much as you are able. We are here for you, Sehywha: our thoughts grow ever closer.

'Yeha Noha.'

I asked the question concerning writing my book about my teachings and travels: would I have enough time left to write all this information (being morbid, I suppose, thinking about the end of my mortal life)? The answer from White Feather was: 'There will be enough time for you to see your work come to fruition, fret not.'

Later that evening, when I had finished our packing, I heard White Feather asking me to sit for a short while.

'We are happy for you to rest, Sehywha, whilst you are by the ocean. One thought each day will keep us connected to you. You already know of the strength of Spirit: it will be even stronger in that place. Whilst you are there we ask that you collect eight large pebbles. Colour does not matter but they should all be of the same dimension. We shall use these in our future learning and will speak more about them in the fullness of time. Together with the pebbles we ask that you bring four gull feathers.' (I thought, What does he want these for?) White Feather laughed and said, 'Most people ask for a stick of rock: this one asks for pebbles and feathers. We are not laughing at you, child, just your bewildered thoughts. To be serious, we would say to you, Enjoy your stay with your family: enjoy the fresh sea air and the feelings you will have in this Spiritual land. We shall be with you and enjoy also. Take time to feel the love of your family around you. Take time to breathe the air and feel the beauty of the land. Listen to the wind in the trees; hear their voices and mind all they say to you.

'Now, child, this one will leave you in peace to make ready for your journey. We will be with you. This you already know. Perhaps this one will ride in your wagon and enjoy the scenery!' White Feather laughed again and said, 'Tell Mon Ami not too many bumps. We shall speak again soon, child.'

(If he is riding in the back of the car I hope he doesn't sit on the Easter eggs!)

We had a super Easter with the family, and as White Feather had advised, did not dwell on the subject of our moving. In actual fact, the subject did come up when Lesley said they had been looking at various properties and pieces of land, but as yet they had not found what they were looking for.

I also managed to find the eight pebbles and four feathers that White Feather had asked me to collect. At a later date I found out that the pebbles would have different symbols painted on them and that the feathers would be used to adorn my 'talking stick'. More about these later...

On my return the following week our lessons began again.

I woke fairly early today, felt White Feather's vibration as soon as I got up.

White Feather: 'Hello, my child, we answer all questions. We are here to guide you and will so do. Your path is already chosen and we will help you to stay on this true path. Sufficient for you to know for now is that we understand mortal life must come first. That is the way of things, Sehywha, learning to live life on Mother Earth. Each day brings both happiness and sadness. There will be times when small problems seem like mountains, but you will overcome.

'Through your mortal life you have suffered much from man's selfishness. You have risen above this and now show your true self. That is why you feel others' pain. You want to help others. Indeed, your very presence helps others to see through their pain, although you do not yet realise this. You do not hear what is said when you leave their presence: we do and would say to you that they feel uplifted when you are with them. This is the power, child, the power of your love for them. Hear my words, Sehywha, and know that what is told is true. Many say that troubled times are when you are being tested in your faith to Spirit: this is not the way of Spirit. Troubled times are Earth- and man-made, there is no test. However, life on Mother Earth is one long test to survive. We know that you understand that we cannot interfere with your mortal life and that, indeed, we would not. Life's problems have to be worked through. Take heart from what these words mean and you will see more clearly. Your awareness grows and as it grows, you feel more intensely. In your words, child, you feel vulnerable. That is why we say to you, Use your shield. This will protect these feelings of vulnerability. We know that sometimes you feel the path is stony; use your gift, child, to look ahead and you will see that the path grows smoother. Now we speak of other matters, Sehywha.

'Keep the pebbles and feathers from your visit, we will show you in the course of time what is needed with these. This is all part of your development, child: we need for you to progress. The gift that is yours cannot be restrained. It must go forward. There is much work you have to do, Sehywha, and all we speak of will help you on your path to understand and to acknowledge these understandings.

'Enough for now, child. We shall speak again soon. Rest well and drink the water. You may receive a pleasant surprise very soon.

'Yeha Noha.'

My sitting with White Feather ended at 8.15 a.m. At 10.45 a.m. Laughing Bear telephoned me with the news that he had made me a medicine shield which he was posting that day.

I duly received the medicine shield, which now hangs on my wall, and it gives me a great feeling of love and joy each time I look at it. It consists of the head and skin of a fox and is bound around the edges with rabbit fur. It has crow and hawk feathers, a claw for defence and an internal sea slug 'skeleton' for journeying. The colours painted on the shield are red for vitality; green for healing and renewal; black for thought, ancestral guidance and beginnings; brown for stamina and strength; and black/white for attraction/repulsion (and attractiveness too). The animals that represent the colours are frog, bear, skunk, elk and lion. The fox is for observation, camouflage and for travelling safely and avoiding hostility. Kerys is also making me a rattle, which will follow later.

The next day I heard White Feather asking me to rise and sit.

White Feather: 'Hello, my dear child, we hope we did not alarm you by our sudden appearance yesterwhile.' (I was busy ironing when I suddenly saw him standing in the kitchen doorway, leaning against the door.) I told him that I was not alarmed, just surprised, as I was thinking of other things.

'We shall show ourself to you much more often, and you will be aware of our presence more easily. We acknowledge that the one called Connie has arrived safely and is at present sleeping. We understand the question with regard to the sleeping state in Spirit. We can say that some sleep through great exhaustion because of their struggle to fight their illness. Some need sleep to be rid of the strong medicine they were given before they passed to Spirit. Strong medicine not only affects the vessel but seeps through to the inner self, the Spirit. We hope that this answers your ponderings, child.'

I told White Feather that I had been aware of children's voices for the last couple of days, mainly laughing and giggling. White Feather said he knew of this. 'Do not be concerned as to why they are with you: these are those we call our precious ones: they are here simply to fill your lodge with love and harmony. All things will come together in the fullness of time. The important matter for you now is to concentrate on your true work. We need you, child, we need you to use the knowledge you have gained from Spirit. So many people need to know more about Spirit. It is true to say that some have a great fear of what they cannot see and feel, so are reluctant to recognise what they may already be receiving from Spirit. Some people even feel that they would be laughed at, if they spoke of their feelings and thoughts. Too many of the old ways are instilled in many and these are their ways: they will not change. But there are those who thirst for knowledge of Spirit. We shall spend a little time each day, child, on our awareness. We shall sharpen our hearing and vision. We know and approve of the process you use to communicate with those other than this one. Whatever you are comfortable with using, child: the method is not important.

'As always, child, we are here. Rest well. We shall speak again soon.

'Yeha Noha.'

The other method I use for communication to those in Spirit is by writing a note or just a few lines to open up the channel between us. I perhaps say something like 'Hi, Mum, how are you, are you busy?' Sometimes the answer comes almost immediately; sometimes I do not hear anything for a few hours, but I do get an answer in one form or another.

Praise from my Guide and a Message for Steve

One way I meditate, which I learned from one of the John Edward tapes I have, is by mentally picturing a room that is mine and mine alone. No one can enter this room: it is my space and mine alone. I myself cannot enter this room until I have deposited all my thoughts of worry and restlessness in the trunk situated outside. Once I have got rid of the junk and put it inside the trunk and closed the lid, a key appears on the trunk lid, which allows me then to open the door to my room.

Inside the room to my right is what I call my communication centre. This consists of a very large TV screen, a pair of speakers and, on the workspace in front of all this, a notepad and pen/pencil. If I stand in the centre of the room and look straight in front of me I have a healing couch and to the left of this there is a window in the shape of a triangle. Still standing in the centre of the room facing the healing couch, I look to my left, at the window that has a thick shutter over it. When the shutter is lifted this window represents my third eye.

On this particular morning after my meditation I felt the need to 'go to my room'. After going through the process of being able to enter, I opened the door and stepped in and noticed that the TV screen was flickering. I sat in front of it and pictures of faces began to appear. So many different people. There were some I recognised, some I did not. These were faces of people who had passed on to Spirit. I saw my nan, granddad, aunts, uncles and friends. One of the faces belonged to a very old friend, a lady by the name of Thelma, with whom I had worked in 1972 and who had passed away in 1973. She had just popped in to say 'hello'. I sat watching the screen. It felt really weird – not scary-weird but a nice feeling. I could hear sounds coming from the speakers, laughter and voices all trying to speak at once. I was aware at this point that White Feather was standing behind me, I felt his hands resting on my shoulders. He didn't speak but was watching the images with me as they came and went. The vision of the lake and mountains suddenly appeared on the screen and then White Feather spoke.

'We are here, child, to thank you for allowing this one to come to your most private place. Do you like what has been done here?' I had not looked at the room itself when I entered: I had been too busy looking at the screen. Now I looked and saw that it had been made into what looked like a sitting room. There were pictures on the walls, mainly scenes of views overlooking hills, streams, the sea and some beautiful flower gardens. There was a small table with a huge vase of flowers of all different colours and varieties, and a very comfortable sofa. White Feather told me to look behind the sofa, which I did. I nearly fell over in surprise... There was our dog Angus, looking very fit, wagging his tail for all he was worth. He was so pleased to see me. I felt the tears beginning to well up: he was a very special dog to both me and to Vic. I also felt very sad because it was I who had taken him to the vet's to be put to sleep. He had cancer and had got to the stage where he just didn't want to get up to eat or go out. He just lay on the floor all the time. The vet had been treating him for some time with medicines, but to no avail. We finally decided that we could not bear to see him suffer any longer but it was down to me to take him on his final journey, Vic said he could not do it. Hence the feeling I had now of sadness. White Feather spoke: 'Do not recall painful memories, Sehywha. Do not blame yourself; your dog does not, so why should you? Your friend will be here whenever you wish to see him.'

I sat on the sofa with Angus at my feet and looked around me. This is really a lovely room: very bright and colourful. I thought about how very lovely it was just to be able to sit there and how great it was that I could come at any time I wished.

'This is your place, child,' White Feather said. 'Use it well to develop your awareness. You already know that you can go to the lake at any time for quiet and to fill your senses with peace. This place will be for work. Here you can speak to whoever show themselves to you. You will know, child, when you need to be here, when messages need to be given. As we have spoken before, the more you meditate, the more you will see, hear and feel. We wish to say to you that we are pleased with the time you spend in Spirit work, but please do remember to dedicate some time to yourself. Your days are filled with chores and your Spirit work, leaving very little time for you to be you. You understand this? Play your music, child. There are many pieces to learn, and in so doing you will find yourself feeling rewarded. Now, child, this one will leave you to enjoy your special place. Remember to mind all that you receive and to write in your working tool. Enough for now, Sehywha. We shall speak again soon.

'Yeha Noha.'

When I was back from this wonderful journey I thanked White Feather for the decoration of my room, the flowers and for bringing Angus. I don't expect to see him there every time I go there but it was so very nice to see him again.

The following day I rose early. I wished to speak to White Feather about a few things Steve had talked to me about the previous evening. I did my meditation and decided to postpone my shower to see if White Feather would speak with me. I sat for about five minutes or so and then heard his voice.

'Hello, my child, we heard our name called, we are here, please to ask questions of this one, we are here to help you. We bring wishes of love and well-being from our friends in Spirit, our brothers and sisters too.' My first question to White Feather concerned Steve and Gwyn selling their house. It had been on the market for quite a while and had not drawn any interest from buyers. When Steve was talking about it I sensed the frustration in his voice.

White Feather: 'Please to tell our young friend that the time is not yet right for him to leave that place. He should wait a while longer; bigger things are to come in due course. We do not have the power to change his path; sufficient for him to know that when the time is right he will be given all the help he needs to accomplish his desires. Patience, all will be well. Tell him to continue with his images (*drawings*), this work goes very well; his readings that accompany the images also. We know how much our young friend wishes to settle: tell him all will become clear in the fullness of time. There are many who surround our young friend. His guides and helpers are with him constantly. Tell him to lift his heart and to quicken his step and know that Spirit is working with him to achieve his heart's desire.

'As with all things, child, you are all mortals, and must follow each path that is laid down for that purpose. The lodge (*Steve's new home*), wherever it may be, will be there for him when the time is right. Matters concerning the well-being of one's own true Spirit must come first. His awareness of Spirit grows very fast; this we know. He has reached a point now when he receives an answer to a question asked before it has been fully given. Images (*drawings*) too are becoming stronger. We know that he is reluctant to so do but he must push himself forward a little more in his Spirit work so that he will be noticed. As with you, dear child, this young friend will work for Spirit full-time: he will not need any other work. His work for Spirit will bring him payment enough so that he can cease his daily toil (*job*). (*Whilst I am writing this for Steve I am seeing a circle of very bright lights – blue, gold, white, purple, all very sharp – dancing just in front of me. Wow!*) Our young friend has much knowledge inside himself that has not shown itself yet. The words we leave you with concerning our young friend are, The best is yet to come.

My other question to White Feather concerned Laughing Bear. I had not heard from him for a while and was concerned. White Feather: 'Similarly we say to you as we have just said to our young friend: patience, child, you will hear from Laughing Bear. He has spent much time in his Spirit work and has somewhat neglected his physical needs. He has much work to do and to this matter he needs much time to readjust himself. We know you understand this, Sehywha; your prayers for his well-being are received with thankfulness. He knows that we are around him and needs no reminding of what we wish of him. We say to you that the day you do not look for him he will be at your door. Take heart from this and go about your daily life. As we have spoken before, a tree does not grow overnight. Water and feed that which grows inside you. Your time for blossoming comes soon and brings with it more happiness than you have ever known. Do you not recognise the feelings inside you when you speak about Spirit to those like-minded (*Steve*) and how your energy surges like a river when the dam has been removed? This is just the beginning, child: imagine what it will be like when you have this feeling constantly. Spirit is truly a wondrous feeling. Now, child, we have spoken enough for this time. Take time to rest, Sehywha. Leave your chores: they are not important for this day. Give yourself some free time. We shall be close by.

'Yeha Noha.'

I have written White Feather's words for Steve and will post it tomorrow. I hope he understands the message.

I had a phone call from Steve a couple of days later, he asked me to thank White Feather for his words. Steve said he was bang on with what he had said. Steve could identify with all that was said to him. I thanked White Feather for his words to Laughing Bear, concerning his (White Feather's) life on Earth, and for guiding me on my Spiritual path.

The next day, after meditation, White Feather asked me to sit for our next lesson. White Feather: 'Hello, my child, we are happy to know our words bring comfort and understanding. Perhaps the knowledge concerning this one will make the bond even stronger between us. We have many roads to travel, Sehywha, much to see and much to learn. We have spoken and you have seen much already. The Spirit world is not a fantasy, child, it is very real. You know this, for have you not been given positive proof? Have you not spoken with and do you not feel family and friends who are no longer on the Earth plane? Laughing Bear is strong in the knowledge of communication between the two of us, but you are also able to communicate with other Spirits, for have you not done so with Abraham? Soon there will be others to help you gain knowledge of all you seek. We know you have questions, child, concerning words written by Laughing Bear. Do not concern yourself: all will become clear in the fullness of time. It is interesting, is it not, that two of the colours given to you by Laughing Bear were already chosen by yourself? Remember the feathers, child, three white and one black: this one will teach you to make these into a tool for good medicine. The pebbles you collected must be cleansed, buried in the earth for seven days, lifted, cleansed again and placed in a leather pouch. When you are ready, child, and you have questions from people who ask, spread the stones before you in a circle, take the shanso (*medicine stick or feathers*) and brush the stones lightly. Wait for images to appear on the surface of the stones.' (*The stones/pebbles White Feather speaks about and the medicine stick are all to do with journeying or walking the shamanic path, about which I will speak later in the book.*)

'Have no fear, little one, for when you journey to the other worlds, this one will be with you. We shall travel together: no harm will come to you. This one has made a promise to guard you against all harm… This promise will be kept.

'As we journey, answers to all questions will be answered. We tread the path of our ancestors, and they too will be happy that your true path has been shown to you. There will be times, child, when you will feel a great tiredness after our journeying. Please to take the time to rest well. We have many surprises to show on our journey. Just remember, Sehywha, all things are possible if you have love and faith.

'Yeha Noha.'

The explanation of White Feather's words concerning Shamanic work, travelling to other worlds, encountering many things I have never even heard of before, was in response to a letter I had received from Kerys Laughing Bear and the things that he had told me concerning my Spiritual path. After reading his letter, I have no doubt in my mind that in one of my 'other lives' on this earth, I was indeed related to White Feather in some form. White Feather sometimes gives me little hints concerning 'family', 'our ancestors', etc. This probably explains the closeness I feel for him and also for Laughing Bear. Sometimes when I am sitting quietly during the day, after I have finished my daily chores, I can hear drumming and sometimes the flute: it makes me feel like I want to get up and dance. Indeed, since I began my shamanic work, I *do* dance; it is all part of the ceremony.

The next day after I had completed my meditation I was in the shower and thinking about everything that had happened over the last couple of years. Thoughts and questions began filling my head and White Feather in his infinite wisdom said, 'Finish your chores, child, and then we shall speak. Come to the lake, the special place.' This I did.

When I arrived White Feather was, as usual, sitting on the ground. He motioned me to sit then turned away and looked at the water. I was eager to talk so began asking questions. White Feather stopped me mid-flow by holding up his hand. He was still looking at the water and not at me. After what seemed like for ever he turned to me and spoke: 'Now, child, we will talk. We know that you have much to speak about but please do not rush your words. We have time a-plenty, there is no reason to be in such a hurry. There are some things that cannot be changed, and although you wish that this were possible, it cannot be. We understand your feelings of regret with regard to time. We hear you say, Why could not this have happened earlier in my life, when I was younger? The simple answer to the question, child, is that you were not ready. We have spoken before, have we not, about life's experiences? You understand the meaning of what is happening now because you have gained the necessary experience and are ready to do your true work. Having spoken those words we wish to add to them by saying that you are learning by experience still. We also wish to say, Do not spend time on matters that cannot be changed. Recognise them and then move on. Concentrate on what you are doing now: your daily life is full at this present time with your writings, your urge to gain knowledge of your ancestry. Do not concern yourself with time so much, my child. Walk, do not run. We hear you say, I have not got much time to do all I want to do, why does time pass so quickly? Time travels at the same pace every day so time is not the problem. Try to understand what this one is saying, Sehywha: you cannot fit four jugs of water into one jug. You understand? Good. You must pace yourself, child, and recognise this fact. Do not concern yourself. All will be well. Just remember to take a little of this precious time to be you. Come to the lake. Let yourself rest and fill your Spirit with this wonderful sight. It is there for you, child: you may come as often as you wish. When you return to your everyday life you will feel refreshed and ready to face whatever lies in your path.

'Now we will speak of other matters. We have spoken to Laughing Bear: he is preparing something for you, as you already know. His medicine will help you, child, on your many travels. Listen to his words, Sehywha: they will give protection and ensure that you return safely from your journeys. Do as he bids. This one is very happy to know that your knowledge of our ancestry grows. It is good that you recognise words and images of our people of long ago. All that you see and feel will slowly bring back to you the old ways – so much so that you will find yourself following them without realising that you are doing so. We know also that you now realise the meaning of the colours. Good. (*Colours refer to red, black, white and yellow: the colours of the human race.*) Reading is a wonderful thing, is it not? (*White Feather is chuckling to himself now.*)

Now, child, we speak of your journey to the river. (*This is in answer to a dream I had spoken to him about. I dreamt that I found myself on the banks of a river, which appeared to be fast-flowing and quite deep. An Indian woman was standing on the opposite side of the river beckoning me to come to her. I wanted to cross to the other side and so looked around for some sort of boat to carry me there. There was no boat: the only way was for me to swim. I like water but I am not a good swimmer and, when swimming, always try to stay within my depth. I looked at the river and thought, There is no way I am going in there! The water was dark and there was no telling how deep. After a while, the woman, realising I was not going to join her, turned and walked away, a little sadly, I felt. Shortly after, I woke up.*)

'The answers you seek, child, are on the other side of the river. To know the answers you must first cross that river. You must have faith and trust in yourself: no harm will come to you if you enter the water. This dreamtime is also a symbol, the meaning of which is thus: Sometimes the things that you want and the answers you need are just that little bit out of reach. To obtain what you desire you must be prepared to go that little bit further. Then and only then will you realise where all this is leading you. If you have thoughts or maybe questions about what you do, give voice to them. Sometimes you will find you have the answers just by asking the questions out loud.

'Now, my dear child, this one will leave you to think on these thoughts. We leave you with one more. As you have said many times yourself, there is a purpose to what you are about, child. Everything has a purpose. Nothing is coincidental. As we have also said many times, all will be revealed in the fullness of time. That time comes soon, child, and to this end you are being prepared. You understand? Good. Yeha Noha.'

I was back before I had asked White Feather if I would dream again about the river. Perhaps if it happens again I will be brave and close my eyes and jump in! Sometimes when I think over the words he speaks I think he is speaking in riddles but, when I take one section at a time, break it up, so to speak, I find that it is honest and does in fact make sense.

Perhaps it was wrong of me, but I began looking forward to going to bed each night, hoping that the Indian lady and the river would be there again. Unfortunately this did not happen, but later, when I was doing my shamanic work and did a partial soul retrieval, I had to face water and did indeed have to swim for it: my life depended on it! If you think that all this is barely believable, wait until you read about my vision and journeying along the Shamanic path.

The following weekend Vic and I visited Glastonbury and the Chalice Well. For anyone who has not visited this place I would heartily recommend that you do. It is so Spiritually uplifting, walking around the gardens, sitting by the Chalice Well head, listening to the water flow. We always take some of the water home with us, both for ourselves and for our friends. Four drops of well water to one glass of tap water every day are recommended to cleanse the inner you. There is also a small pool that is called the foot spa: you stand in this and even on the hottest day the water is absolutely freezing. I have had trouble with my feet since I was a child so I always take advantage of the foot spa whenever we visit and, I must say, I feel the benefit of it. Wherever you go around the gardens you will find little arbours where you can sit and meditate. It really is a lovely place. On one of our visits we were privileged to see Tim Wheater and listen to his wonderful music and chanting. It is a truly special place to visit.

The following Monday morning White Feather asked me to sit. 'Hello, my child, we will not stay long, we know you have many chores to do (*had been sorting dirty washing for machine*) and that you wish to complete them before the sun gets too high in the sky (*having a heat wave at the moment*). It is good that you visited the waters (*Glastonbury*); many people over the years have trod the path to take these waters. There is no doubt that there are healing powers there. The healing comes from deep inside Mother Earth and to all that come to this place for healing, healing will be given. We see the writings, Sehywha: they are growing daily. Do not be deterred by the time they take. We know that as you write you relive our talks and journeys together. Many things come to mind as you do this: little things that you realise were not on the paper and therefore must be added. Do not rush, child; it is more important that the words are meaningful and that it is clear to those who read them. Now you know why we say that this is your working tool and why it is important for you to write all that you see, hear and feel. Observation is very, very important but we know we do not have to speak of this, for already you are knowing. Some take all of their earthly lives to complete one writing task, but you have the advantage of our many talks to refer to. Yes, Sehywha, prayers to the Great Spirit are answered. The answers may not come today or tomorrow but they will come. He knows your prayers, child, and knows what is in your heart. Time spent in prayer uplifts the soul and sometimes by praying you answer your own questions and problems. Suffice to say to you that all you do now also helps this one. It gives this one the knowledge that we are, in your words, "doing our job right"! This is how it should be. Not many people today would take the time to listen to a person of 180 years or take their words and live as that person showed them. We have come a long way together, Sehywha, and the knowledge of this and all you do makes this one very happy.

'Enough sentiment now, child: it is not good for our connection to allow emotion to enter. The channel will become cloudy and this we do not need. Suffice for you to know that all is as it should be. We shall speak again soon, Sehywha.

'Yeha Noha.'

After White Feather had left I sat thinking about all he had said and I felt quite elated, as if I had gotten good marks from my teacher. I mustn't let it go to my head, but I have to admit I felt very uplifted. These are the rewards for my Spiritual work: words of praise from my guide and mentor. Needless to say I swept through my chores that day on cloud nine!

A few days later when we visited a couple of our Spiritually minded friends and were discussing the many conversations and teachings I had received from White Feather, I asked if they knew what a rainbow warrior was. I knew of the Greenpeace ship that has this name but apart from that knew very little of what a rainbow warrior actually was. The following morning I heard White Feather calling me to sit to 'discuss matters' (his words), which I duly did.

'Hello, my child, we wish to speak about the path you travel and the many experiences you will encounter on your journey. We see and hear all in your many conversations and meetings with like-minded people. We are not, as such, a philosopher. Although some of our words may carry a philosophical tendency; this is merely meant for understanding purposes only. Your path as a rainbow warrior will be a difficult one to tread at times. In these hard times we need you to remember why you follow this path.

'We have spoken before, have we not, about your earthly journey? You are a Spiritual warrior, a peace keeper of ancient traditions, and as such you will teach the people how to walk in peace and live in unity with one another. There are many who tread this path, child: you are not the only one who carries the voices of the ancient ones. Unfortunately there are those amongst you who have chosen to ignore these voices and teachings. Within each rainbow warrior's heart lies the eternal flame of hope and love for all two-legged, four-legged, winged and finned alike.

'We hear your thoughts, child. You ask, How can I achieve all this? The answer is simple. All images and thoughts that come to you, put down on paper for your project (*book*). Soon the images and thoughts come together to form a picture. Remember the jigsaw, Sehywha, one piece at a time until the whole picture becomes clear?

'We know that your heart is filled with love for the Creator (*God*) and for all his children. Call the Creator what you will – God, Creator, Great Spirit – he is one and the same. Remember, child, he walks beside each and every one of his children, wherever they are. He is all around, everywhere, there is nothing that comes to you that is not of him. You may call his name whatever and whenever.

'The Creator has chosen you amongst many to understand the connection to Mother Earth. She sustains you and needs all people to work together to help heal her. People must be told that they cannot keep taking and taking from her. Something must be put back or she will perish. We know you understand our words, child, and are willing to walk the path of the unjust and greedy to show the way, the Path of Enlightenment. Your project when completed will show that life on Mother Earth can be a better place. Praying for those with negative thoughts may seem a hard thing to do but it must be done. Forget vengeance and retaliation. The presence of the rainbow warriors will teach people to pray, to speak and live in harmony, and to treat Mother Earth with respect, taking only what is needed to replace what is taken from her and, as always, thanking her for sustaining us. Thus some of the imbalance may be restored. Everything moves in a circle, child, there is no beginning and no end, just perfect harmony.

'We see your quest for knowledge, Sehywha, and that it grows stronger. It is good that you read and learn.

'To go forward on your path strongly and fully committed to what you do, you must take time to retrace your steps, to seek the truth of your ancestry and who you are. This you are so doing, quenching your thirst for all you need to know, thus giving you the learning for your Spiritual work.

'We shall leave you in peace now, child. We are, as always, just a thought away.

'Yeha Noha.'

White Feather's last comment before he left was said with a laugh: 'Tell our friend to look at his own reflection before he comments on Sehywha's nose.'

This last comment came as a bit of a shock to Vic. The previous evening we had been talking and I'm not sure how it came up but I commented on someone's nose – a picture in a magazine, I think – and Vic said something like, 'You can talk! What about your nose? It's a right cherry picker.' So you see, there is absolutely nothing that goes on in our conversations that is missed by our guides. I think that White Feather has a really good sense of humour, which he has shown on several occasions.

I thought about all White Feather had said concerning being a rainbow warrior and what it entailed and about my commitment to this. I am still not sure just how this is going to come about: maybe it will have an effect on people after they read these words of White Feather. Believing in something and doing it for yourself is one thing. To get other people to think along the same lines is quite another.

Although it has been a while since I wrote in this book of White Feather's daily teachings, he is still with me, advising me as I travel along life's way. All of these teachings are now being put into a book form and I write as often as possible. Today, just as I began to pick up my writings, I heard White Feather call me to go to the lake to speak.

'Hello, my child. Thank you for hearing our call to sit. We know you are understanding of reasons why we do not ask you to sit every day. The book goes well. It is important that you finish this, Sehywha, with little or no distractions. We also understand your yearning for knowledge regarding the old ways. We are happy that you so do. Do not take too much on yourself at one time. This will drain your energy. By all means, follow the shamanic path. This is good. To teach the ways of the shaman you must first learn all there is to know about them. It is good that you seek guidance with this because it will be a hard path to tread, with many sacrifices along the way. You must come to the lake at regular intervals to replenish lost energy and to give yourself some quiet time. We are knowing of your concerns and would say to you, Do not believe everything you hear. It is a sad way of your world that gestures of help and healing offered to those in need can be taken and twisted into something they are not. Our friend is receiving help from his guides and mentors; do not concern yourself, all will be shown in the fullness of time. We wish to say also, Do not spend your energy speaking cross words over this matter. You know the truth: let it lie.

'Now, child, we wish to speak of other matters. It was pleasing to this one to hear the words of the one they call "Richard". Listen to his words, Sehywha, for have we not spoken of those matters when we first began our talking? You are too self-critical. Recognise yourself for what you are: believe in yourself. Once you have walked the way of the shaman you will have the answers you seek. Use this learning, Sehywha. It will make you stronger in Spirit. In return for your continued work for Spirit and the understandings you have, you will be given the purest of love for all around you. Once you wear the cloak of the fox you will be able to travel unseen wherever and whenever you like. Your journeys will open up a wider image of what is to come. We have one word of warning here, child: do not push too hard. All will come to you in the fullness of time. We shall be with you and, unless asked, will not interfere in any way. Just know of our presence and that we will assist you with the power you need for your journeying. Just as you hear the rattle and drum when this one calls to you, so shall you use the same to call this one when you feel the need. It is a brave thing that you do, child: many would not want to tread this path. Their fear of the unknown would hold them back. We are understanding of why you need to tread this path and make the promise to you that, when you reach the end of your journeys, a most pleasant surprise awaits you, and this surprise will answer every question that you have had concerning your ancestry and the link between this one and yourself. Enough for now, child: we are ever near, and just a thought away.

'Yeha Nona.'

One other matter I would like to talk about here, and that is the appearance of Woody in my life. Woody is a beautiful wood pigeon and he suddenly appeared one day, at the start of my shamanic work. He sits on top of the telegraph pole in my garden and also comes onto the shed roof. When I sit at the kitchen table I can see him and when I open the curtains in the mornings he is there, usually on the pole, and I always acknowledge him. I say, 'Good morning, Woody.' He looks at me and sometimes answers me with his call. There is also a 'Mrs Woody' and on occasions she joins her mate, sitting alongside him balancing on the actual telephone wire.

One of the many experiences I would like to share with you concerning Woody is as follows.

One evening, around dusk, Woody was still sitting on his pole so I went out to speak with him. I said, 'Isn't it about time you went to bed? It will be dark soon.' Woody stared straight at me and then a most amazing thing happened. He lifted his wings from the shoulders, pushed his head forward and then started to get bigger. I could not take my eyes from what I was seeing. Woody became an eagle, with a hooked beak and yellow eyes. He looked straight into my eyes and gave me a feeling of absolute happiness and trust. After what seemed like ages but in fact was just seconds, he began to shrink back to his normal size.

I spoke to Merlynne, my shamanic teacher, about this episode and this is the explanation she gave me. Woody was showing me how much I had changed. The eagle is the most sacred animal to the First Nations of America. He carries our prayers to the Great Spirit and returns 'his' messages to us. The eagle has great healing powers and brings the medicine of the Teacher. Merlynne concluded by saying that there may be great things in store for me in the future. How wonderful!

Woody sometimes appears during the day and always comes to say goodnight before he flies off to the fir tree where the Woodys have their home.

I have grown very fond of Woody and know that he is there for a reason. I was told by White Feather that Woody would be with me as a helper whilst I followed the shamanic path, to give me inspiration with my writing as well. To date Woody has been with me since September 2003, nearly two years. I hope he stays once I have finished writing this book. He did disappear for a while once I had completed my shamanic course. He was away for a couple of weeks and I thought to myself, That's it, he is gone, you won't see him again. Well, I was wrong. He suddenly appeared on a Sunday morning, bedraggled and weary. I immediately went to speak to him, asking him where he had been and what he had been up to. Poor thing, he did look sorry for himself. After a few days he returned to his favourite perch: we put some food out for him on the shed roof and he began to look like his old self.

I asked myself why he had returned. I thought his visits would stop once my course had finished. I suddenly felt very strongly that although my course was completed I still had work to do on writing my book, and that was the reason Woody had returned.

This morning both Mr and Mrs Woody have been for their 'breakfast' and gave us a demonstration, a little dance in the sunshine. Because of the awareness that White Feather has awoken in me I seem to understand Woody's messages, and not just his, but those from other birds, as well. We have quite a few bird feeders and a bird table that we keep topped up, and if for any reason I have to go into the garden, perhaps to the dustbin, I can hear Bobby the robin telling me off. He is saying, 'Go back indoors. I want to eat and I cannot come down whilst you are there.'

As I said before, if you care to listen, it is all there for you. It is all part of Mother Nature.

Travelling the Shamanic Path

As you will have gathered from the last conversation with White Feather, I have decided the time has come for me to commence my shamanic work. To this end I have enrolled on a course with Merlynne White Bear.

When I first started I had no idea what was involved or that I would be able to follow this course until the finish. It was extremely hard work but thoroughly enjoyable. I was very grateful for all the help that I received from Spirit. I know that they helped me and that I could not have done it alone. I found the work absolutely fascinating. I learned about the directions and their meanings, the animals that represent the directions and the Spirits, too. I also learned about the seasons, the solstices and the different elements that represent the directions and their meanings.

I studied the crystals and their meanings, the tarot and the runes. I went out into the countryside, looked at and felt different trees and listened to their voices as they spoke to me while the wind blew through their branches. I touched and communicated with different flowers and watched the ducks on the lake as they dived for food. I watched, listened and felt nature, as I had never done before. One of the exercises I had to do was to sit somewhere quiet, with just a few passers-by in close proximity, eyes closed, listening for their footsteps, trying to identify with my third eye as to their attire. It is amazing just what you can pick up when someone walks by you, someone who you cannot see at that moment. You can visualise whether they are male or female and use your sense of smell to pick up perfume or if they are a smoker or even if they are unwashed.

By experiencing all these different things I started to realise that there was another world out there. Ordinary daily chores such as cleaning, cooking, ironing etc., seem very mundane after spending time with my shamanic work. In order to fit everything in, I decided I would have to have some sort of routine. I started making a list of daily chores to be done and what I needed to do with my shamanic work. It is quite remarkable just what you can accomplish in a day. To fully appreciate what I was being taught, with all that I had to learn in walking the shamanic path, I had to commit myself to at least one whole day per week for study, one day for ceremony and some time for my drum work and for dancing.

It took me a while but I managed to get myself into a regular pattern. Whilst doing my shamanic work I made sure that I unplugged the telephone just in case I was interrupted and that I was not expecting any callers – for example the window cleaner. At first, after trying to juggle everything so that I could fit all my different areas of work in, I felt very tired. Some days I longed for bedtime so that I could just sleep. But after a few weeks I realised that everything was falling into place, as it were, and that my tiredness was lifting.

One thing for which I am grateful to White Feather is the lesson he gave me in smudging. He showed me how to make smoke with what I thought at the time was a bunch of heather: in actual fact he was showing me how to smudge myself to cleanse away negativity.

To give you a rough idea of what shamanic healing entails, I will write a little about my experiences. First I will explain what a shaman believes. A shaman sees sickness in a person as a loss of power, as a loss of one's soul or part of it. When we are healthy and have our whole soul we are powerful and, being powerful, are able to repel any negative energies (or bad Spirits). When our soul becomes fragmented and we only have part of it, we are vulnerable to invasion from illness and disease.

At some time in our lives nearly all of us go through a traumatic experience one way or another. It is then that we feel lost and unable to cope, and powerless against feelings of downheartedness or dispiritedness. It is the duty of the shaman to go and search for this missing piece of the soul and return it to its rightful owner, thus allowing the 'patient' to feel whole and well again. The journey that the shaman takes to recover this fragmented piece is not always a simple one. As you may recall, Kerys Laughing Bear told me about the possibilities of being hurt and even bleeding.

To find our patient's missing piece of soul we have to journey to the lower world, which lies beneath us.

Brief explanation: to get to the lower world, you travel downwards. The entrance could be at a base of a tree or a hole in the bank of a river. When you enter you begin to feel yourself descending further and further. Lower world is very dark, smells musty and dank and is inhabited by all manner of what I call slimy creatures.

Middle world: this is where we are now, where we live.

Upper world: this is the Spiritual realm.

For my shamanic work I have my tools. These consist of, amongst other things, a drum. My husband purchased an unpainted one from a drum-maker in the USA, which I then exchanged with Kerys for a decorated one made out of deerskin. There is a picture of a buffalo on mine. This drum, before it came to me, had been well 'powered-up' by Kerys, as he had taken it to many Spiritual places and used it in ceremony. The drum was used at Stonehenge inside the stones, in a drumming spiral dance at sunrise and in a dreamwish ceremony. It had been used at Glastonbury for circle ceremony, at Avebury, at Men on Toll, at West Kennet long barrow, and underground in an ancient burial chamber: this was as a preparation for journeying. So you see, I have a very powerful drum to use for my ceremonies.

My other tools consist of a rattle – once again I am honoured as this was a gift from Kerys which he had hand made; a tail feather which once belonged to an African fish eagle; a fan made from the feathers of a snowy owl; an assortment of crystals and coloured stones; and four large clear crystals which I place at the four corners of my patient's chair.

Now that I have explained roughly what shamanic work entails and the tools I use, I will tell you a little about two of my journeys that I took.

One journey I took was to meet with my 'power animal': that is, the animal that would accompany me on my many journeys to the lower world.

I was lying in my circle, facing south. My impressions were vague at first: all I knew was that I was in a forest or wood somewhere and that it was autumn. All around me were leaves of yellow, brown and red. I felt someone watching me but could not see anyone. I finally saw a shy creature peering at me from behind a tree. It was a beautiful amber-coloured fox that blended in with the fallen leaves. For some reason I felt that it was a 'he'. It was his eyes that held my attention. He looked at me for a while, then disappeared. I had to do this exercise a few times before he actually stayed with me for a while. On the fifth night after my exercise I went to bed and went directly to sleep. Some time later I was awoken by what I thought was a dog yelping. The yelping got closer and closer and eventually it came from beneath my window in the garden. There were three foxes in the garden, looking like a family. In all the twelve years we had lived here we had never seen a fox, even though we are in the countryside.

The following morning I set my circle up early and began my meditation. I heard White Feather telling me to speak to the fox when he appeared, to ask him if he wished to speak with me.

I am in the wood again, leaves lying as before. Fox appears. I ask him not to run away and assure him that I mean him no harm. Fox comes close to me: I can smell him, I can feel his breath on me. Fox looks at me then turns away. Taking a few steps, he looks back: he wants me to follow him. I follow him to the edge of the wood, where we face a field of what looks like corn or wheat. This confuses me for a moment because in the wood it seems like autumn or winter, in which case corn would not be growing at the same time. I decide not to question what I am being shown as it does not feel to be of any significance.

Fox sits down and then lowers himself onto his belly in a crouching position. He looks at me so I do the same. He starts to move forward slowly, looking back at me to do likewise. We are weaving our way through the corn in this position, sometimes sitting up to see over the corn.

Men appear (four of them), each one carrying a long stick that look like a spear without the tip. Each one of the men, who are Native American Indians, wears a different headdress of an animal. One has a buffalo head, one a wolf, one an eagle and the last one a bear.

We are back in the wood. Fox looks at me and I hear the word 'camouflage' and 'see without being seen'.

Fox has become my totem animal and accompanies me on my journeying. He is what I call my main animal: there are others but the fox is my main animal friend.

My tutor, Merlynne White Bear, has suggested that I read a book called *Animals Speak* by Ted Andrews, who has written a lot about fox medicine. Fox brings clear vision and hearing, clairvoyance and clairaudience. He is a balance of masculine and feminine energy and marks a change of some sort. He is a wonderful ally to have.

So now that I have my power animal, I have someone to accompany me on my many journeys.

A short time later my tutor asked me if I was aware of my power animal around me. I knew that the fox was around: I heard his cries at night and had found his imprints in the garden. I am aware of him Spiritually when I am sitting in meditation because I have felt him brush against my legs, letting me know that he is there.

Since this time I have travelled many times with him; he is very comforting to be with and listens patiently to all my chatter.

On my return from journeying I sit quietly, thinking about where I have just been and what I have seen. Whilst other people have cats and dogs for company, I have a fox. How wonderful, I say to myself. How much more am I going to find on this exceptional shamanic path?

I do not think that I have ever been scared or frightened of anything or any place I have been shown. I have felt a little apprehensive at times: I think the worst was when I went seeking a fragment of my own soul, about which I will speak shortly.

The main thing that I want to emphasise here is that by enrolling on this course I have embarked on a new path. Following the shaman's way has, in a sense, stirred something inside me. I cannot explain what this feeling is exactly, only that whenever I am following the rituals such as making my ceremonial circle, burning my herbs, drumming, dancing, or anything connected with this path, it feels as if it is not the first time. Perhaps I have been here before: perhaps I am in some way connected or related to White Feather. It may sound a bit presumptuous of me, but everything connected to what I call the 'old ways' seems to come as second nature to me.

These thoughts have filled my head for a while so no doubt White Feather is, as always, one step ahead of me. On two occasions he has spoken to me in his own language, Shoshoni. My husband sent for a Shoshoni language book, together with a Lakota dictionary. My next sitting with White Feather confirmed that we had done the right thing in getting these books, as you will see.

I felt like a lie-in this morning but knew I needed to get up and prepare for a message from White Feather. As soon as I had finished my meditation he was there, not with his usual 'Hello, child' but with new words.

White Feather: *'Haganni naha mehwe daoda shoshoni.'* (He is laughing, very loud and for a long time.) 'My little joke, Sehywha: just as well you have your book of words so that you can speak our language. Take one word a day, child, repeat that word over and over whilst you attend to your chores. Soon one word will grow into two, then three, then four. Learn the words that you need to know for ceremony. When you use your drum say the words in our language. Pretty soon you will be saying "thank you" in Shoshoni without realising it.' (He is laughing again.) 'We shall leave you now, child. Know that we are with you and for ever shall be. We shall speak again soon, Sehywha.

'Yeha Noha.'

After I had finished writing I looked up and saw him standing in the doorway to the lounge, in his full regalia. He looked magnificent.

Later I looked up the words he had spoken in Shoshoni. Roughly translated it means, 'How are you finding the Shoshoni language?'

I have chosen the word 'thank you' for my first learning, which in Shoshoni is *aishen.*

Since this time I have learned quite a few words, although I still haven't managed to speak them with the emphasis in the right place. Shoshoni is a hard language to learn, and as long as I have the words I need for ceremony it appears to be enough. White Feather has not told me otherwise. When I mark my circle, it is a *gooni* in Shoshoni. My given name Red Fox is *Ainga Waahni.* I am still learning.

Towards the end of my course I began shamanic healing. I found that as well as using different tools – i.e. drum, rattle and feather – I also needed to listen to what the person I was healing was saying. There is a lot of healing that can be given by just talking together. Indeed,

I have found that most of my healing work is dominated by counselling the client.

I suppose that talking a problem through is a kind of healing. Listening to someone talk about their problems gives meaning to the old adage 'A problem shared is a problem halved', because it helps alleviate that problem. The other healing that is given, for illness or disease, is called soul retrieval. This does not pertain to the whole soul, but just a fragment or part. It is the shaman's job to journey to other worlds to find this lost part of their soul. Once the shaman has located it he returns, carrying it very carefully to his patient, then blows into the heart area of the patient. Sometimes it works well and the patient is restored to good health. Sometimes it has to be done again because, for one reason or another, the fragment does not wish to remain. It could be that the fragment is afraid and wishes to return to the place where it was first located by the shaman.

This is a brief description of soul retrieval. The only other thing that I will say is that the fragment can appear to the shaman as just about anything, from a small boy to an animal. I think the best way of telling you is to describe my own retrieval. That way you may understand better. Here goes.

When my father passed away fourteen months after my mother's death, I could not go to his funeral. I could not face it, nor the fact that he was no more. I had only just recovered from Mum's passing. Vic went and took my daughter Lesley with him. At the time I felt relieved: I would not have to see his coffin or stand in a cold church with grieving relatives. I expect you will think me a coward but, at the time, I just could not do it. It has only been since my involvement with Spirit that I have had pangs of regret about not having said goodbye to him. I prayed to him asking for his forgiveness, and I have since been given proof that he has forgiven me and told me to forget about it and move on. However, this has not satisfied my inner self. I have always felt that something was missing. So, when I discovered that it was possible to do a soul retrieval with anyone, even myself, I decided to journey to find my missing piece.

This is my journey.

I smudged the room, myself and my special place. When this was completed I called on the four directions, above, below and within (seven in all). I put on my multiple drumming CD: this has a fifteen-minute or thirty-minute journey time and has call-back. By doing this, my hands were then free for my rattle and fan. I lay down on my mat.

I am walking through a forest. A large oak tree seems to be calling to me. At the far side of the tree is a small opening just big enough to squeeze through. I enter. It is very slippery underfoot and smells musty. I am descending quite quickly, trying not to slip. It is getting darker. I reach the bottom. It would appear that I am in some kind of cave or grotto. There is a small pool. I can hear water dripping. In the centre of the pool is a large lily pad that looks more like a huge rhubarb leaf than a lily pad. There is a shaft of light coming from above, not very bright, just enough for me to make out a small dog or puppy lying on the leaf. The puppy is light in colour and it is crying. How to reach it? For reach it I must; this is what I have been seeking: my fragment. I feel a warm presence next to my right leg and look down. Fox is here. He nudges me toward the water. Suddenly, the pool is full of water snakes of all different sizes. I shudder: I cannot stand snakes, but I know if I am going to get the puppy from where he is to the shore safely, I must be brave and face them. I hear my guide's voice: 'Sing to them, child, sing your song.'

I open my mouth but nothing comes out: my mouth and throat are dry. I try again and start to sing my song, softly at first and a little squeakily, and then with all my heart I sing as loudly as I can. The snakes stop their thrashing: they just seem to be lying on top of the water, as if asleep. I step into the water and take two steps: the snakes start to move again, coming toward me. I realise it is because I have stopped singing. It is going to be very hard singing and swimming at the same time, but sing I must if I am to avoid being bitten. Again I start to sing and decide to wait a little before entering the water again. I sing like I have never sung before; I cannot tell you how terrified I am. I feel hot and sweaty.

Fox is nudging me again. I look into his eyes: they say, 'Go, go now.' I enter the water. It is not as cold as I had expected. It is very difficult to sing and swim at the same time because I have to keep my head out of the water. The lily pad seems so far away. I push my panic aside and ask my guide for strength. My arms feel tired. I continue to sing and find that I am adding more words to my song, praising the snakes for their protection of the puppy, thanking them for allowing me to enter their pool. I reach the pad and lift the shivering, whining puppy into my arms. I keep singing and include in my song words to the puppy, reassuring him he will come to no harm. I tell him I am taking him somewhere he will be loved and that he will be safe.

Now for the tricky bit! To swim with one hand whilst holding the puppy in the other, and sing!

I again call on my guide for his help: I feel that I am not going to make it back to shore safely. I am determined to fight if needs be to get this puppy back safely. My guide's reply is unbelievable. He pulls on a long chain at the end of which is what looked like a huge plug. The water begins to disappear. I start to move toward the shore, still singing. The water is receding fast but the snakes are still there, thousands of them all squirming over each other. I am now standing only ankle-deep. I move quickly, still singing, to the bank of the pool. As soon as I step onto the bank the pool begins to fill again. No sign of the snakes now. I can hear the water as it flows and cascades into the pool. Suddenly at the far end of the pool a rainbow appears. I thank the snakes again, although I cannot see them. I hold my precious charge close to my heart, soothing him with my voice.

It is still very slippery on the slope going back but the fox is by my side, brushing my legs with his tail. It begins to get lighter: I can see the opening ahead of me. Almost there. As we reach the outside of the oak tree I say goodbye to fox, thanking him for his help. I thank my guide for all his help. I thank the oak tree for guiding me to the lower world.

I hold the puppy as I lie down on my mat, hold him in my cupped hands and blow him gently into my heart. I shake my rattle gently so as not to frighten him as he sinks into my chest. I feel for my fan at my side and gently smooth myself so that all goes well. The call-back on the CD returns me to my surroundings. I lie still, remembering all that has happened to me in the space of half an hour. I suddenly see my father standing in front of me. He hands me a beautiful rose: it is cream with pink edging. He says: 'I have taken all the thorns off so you will not hurt yourself,' then he is gone. I cry with sheer happiness. This means everything to me.

I closed my circle, thanking all who had attended and helped me. I smudged myself, just in case I had picked up any adverse or negative energies.

I realise how lucky I am. First, because I did not think that my first attempt at soul fragment retrieval would be so successful. Secondly, I felt that I had a lot of help from my guide, Senga. Senga is the guide I have who journeys with me. He is a warrior of sorts, a tracker, a scout. My dear friend the fox, who seems to come to me more and more; my main guide/teacher White Feather, who is for ever telling me that I underestimate my capabilities and to believe in myself more: all have helped me so much.

I can honestly say that the whole experience left me feeling very happy and contented and also filled me with awe.

I know that we have to allow time before we know if the fragment retrieved has been successfully reunited with the soul, however (at the time I wrote this in my diaries it had been eight days since I journeyed) I did feel much calmer, slept better and knew that I could carry on with life's path without looking back on this episode with regret.

A little explanation here concerning my song.

Every shaman has his/her own song. It is personal to the shaman and is an expression of the power within him/herself. The shaman's song is also a holy song, one that is evoked by the rhythm of the rattle and drum. It is something that comes naturally to a shaman and cannot be composed like a songwriter with pen and paper. As the shaman progresses the song may change, growing with them as they themselves grow. The shaman's song is given to the shaman by Spirit.

My song was given me by Spirit in a journey I took to find my song. The whole journey took two hours and twenty minutes.

Since I was first given my song it has grown and grows with me still as I walk the shamanic path. As this song is a personal thing to me, it is something that cannot be shared.

My Spiritual work grows also. My daily contact with White Feather continues to teach me; he never ceases to amaze me with his words of wisdom. I have so much to be thankful for that words cannot describe my thoughts. Although Kerys Laughing Bear is still in New Zealand at this time, he is still close to me. I feel it especially when I see a crow perched on the telephone wire looking at me. It is then I know that Kerys is OK and that he has sent the crow with the message. Someone once said if you make a friend of an Indian, you will have a friend for life. I certainly hope so!

White Feather has taught me to respect Mother Earth and all things that dwell thereon. He has taught me how to listen to the words of the trees and flowers and even the grass that grows has something to say. He has taught me to look at the animals, to really watch their movements, the way they stand or sit, the way they hold their heads, and I find myself understanding more and more about these wonderful creatures.

He has shown me many places that are so beautiful and tranquil that they actually bring a lump to my throat. These are the times that I feel I do not want to leave these places, but White Feather reminds me that I still have my life on Earth to live, but when the time comes for me to leave this Earth I will return to these special places, to live my Spiritual life amongst all my relations and friends who already dwell there.

I believe that everyone has the capability to sit in the quiet and learn to communicate with his/her guides and teachers. Most certainly I have many people to thank for making me aware that there is much more to living than just going through the days, rushing here and there – what I call being on a treadmill. This life is for learning, learning the good and the bad, so that you can take all your knowledge with you when you leave. The lessons that you have learned in this life will enable you to help others in the next. The main thing is to know that there is something other than this earthly life and that there is a reason for everything that happens to you whilst you are here. There is a pattern; if you look hard enough you will discover it.

I now know that my path on Mother Earth had already been set out from the day I was born, probably even before. I also know that I have made many mistakes in my life, but as White Feather has said many times, if you do not make mistakes you do not learn. Every time I make a mistake now, I think to myself that I needed to learn that particular lesson, and then I move on.

Now that I have come to the end of my writings I hope that you have enjoyed reading about the many happenings with my guide, White Feather, and myself, about fox and all my animal friends. I hope one day that I will indeed visit Montana and meet up with my 'other' family, the Shoshoni people, and see where White Feather once lived long ago. I have felt the calling many times and indeed have seen it written on paper. When the time is right I shall be there.

Until that time I shall continue to walk the shamanic path, helping others that I meet along the way with their problems, and hopefully pass on all the information that has been given to me from Spirit, so that others may benefit also.

I am still learning about life and the meaning of everything that happens, from day-to-day matters to what I call big events that occur on a worldwide basis.

Mitakoye Oyasin (All our Relations).

One last message.

On 20 April 2005, shortly after I had finished this book, I heard White Feather calling me to the lake as he wished to speak with me.

When I arrived, White Feather was sitting by the water, quietly singing and rocking himself to and fro. I waited until he had finished his song. He patted the ground next to him so I sat down.

White Feather looked long and hard at me, then said: 'Now that the writings are completed, Sehywha, we wish to talk about payment for this, as and when it reaches its final stage. (*I took this to mean once the book had been published.*) Any material gain from your project should be directed toward helping our people in their struggle to exist.

'My child, we know that this may disappoint you, knowing that you will not see any financial benefit for all your hard work. We also know that you, being you, will not question this one's words. However, we feel a little explanation will help you to understand.

'You already know of what we call "give away" and the concept of paying forward, do you not? Good. The benefit to you will come knowing that you are helping our people in their daily living. In turn, recognition for your gift to them will bring into being your heart's greatest desire. You understand? Once the wheel starts to spin, child, many, many things will come your way. Your gifts will be aplenty, taking all manner of wonderful forms, thus giving you much joy. This one, my dear child, knows you will be more than, how you say, "over the moon" with all you receive. No further words are necessary.'

After White Feather had finished speaking, he raised his right hand and drew a large circle. The circle appeared to be a ring of what looked like a smoke trail. He pointed east and a stack of what looked like silver coins appeared. He pointed south and two women appeared. One was myself; the other lady I did not recognise. We were shaking hands and greeting each other like long-lost friends. White Feather's hand moved to the west, and a large jet plane appeared. He raised his hand to the north and an Indian village appeared alongside what looked like an old-fashioned fort with the letter 'W' in front of it. I sat looking at this picture for a while and then White Feather waved his hand and it disappeared.

White Feather: 'Mind what you have been shown, child, and remember. This one will walk at your side when you meet and greet our people and will rejoice in your happiness.

'Yeha Noha.'

The message that White Feather has given me is clear: any remuneration from the sale of this book must be used for the good of the people.

I have decided to donate this money to Lakota Aid, which is a charity run by a lady called Brenda Aplin who lives in Exeter, Devon. This lady works very hard to raise money for the Lakota people so that they can have warm homes in winter, food and medicine for the sick and clothing for the children.

Printed in the United Kingdom
by Lightning Source UK Ltd.
124229UK00001B/76-123/A

9 781844 017171